A Day In My Shoes

A Day In My Shoes

Emily Shipman

Library of Congress Control Number:		2011902911
ISBN:	Hardcover	978-1-4568-7433-9
	Softcover	978-1-4568-7432-2
	Ebook	978-1-4568-7434-6

This book was printed in the United States of America.

To order additional copies of this book, contact:
Xlibris Corporation
1-888-795-4274
www.Xlibris.com
Orders@Xlibris.com
87689

Contents

Chapter One
Winter 2000-2001

December 24, 2000

My name is Emily Rebecca Shipman. I am thirteen and in the seventh grade. I am a very active, fun-loving, outdoor girl! I can't stand sitting around all day!

I have enough problems paying attention as it is for seven hours during my school day. I have a bad case of ADHD. I like to say that I have the attention span of a small rodent. It's true! I can't concentrate on one thing for more than fifteen minutes when I'm sitting down. That's why my favorite class is gym. I get to run. There's also lunch, but there's not as much time there because we have to go through the line, eat, and try to socialize, all within a half hour.

My favorite kinds of music to listen to are hip-hop, a little rap, and some country. Rock is great too. I can't stand classical or opera. Classical makes me feel way out of place. I am definitely not that damn sophisticated. Opera makes me want to hurt people! Why in the hell would anyone enjoy hearing such loud and obnoxious singing?

Onto my favorite color; it's purple. Purple also happens to be one of my high school colors. I won't be going there for another two years, but I'm still looking forward to it a lot.

Italian food is my favorite. I will eat pretty much any kind of pasta dish you set in front of me. I really love it when I get to go to an authentic Italian restaurant and have their salads, and most of the time, the breadsticks are good, but sometimes, they taste a little funny. If you are asking, yes, I do have Italian in my blood, and also French and Irish. If you were also wondering, yes, my family is Catholic. Unfortunately, because of a chromosome issue, we are a little smaller than your average modern Catholic household. Regardless of the circumstances, my parents still live by the rules of the church. We go to mass every week and on holy days of obligation. Most of all, we believe that Jesus drank wine, not grape juice, so raise your glasses to that!

Today, of course, is Christmas Eve, and it is 2:09 p.m. I am singing in the choir tonight at the five-thirty Mass. I also have a really long wish list this year, and as far as I know, I am on Santa's nice list, so I'm hoping to get most of the things.

Now my family and I (meaning my parents and my brother) are on our way to Mass. I stopped writing for a few minutes so I could take a shower and get ready. I can't be stinky going into church, especially when my monthly friend is visiting. This is only the second time. It came for the first time on the first of last month, when I was at school of all things! Eight days before my thirteenth birthday! Happy birthday to me! Not!

Back to Christmas and the Christmas activities now. My Gamma and Gampa Shipman are coming tomorrow for our big feast. They are also bringing us some presents.

Well, not much else for now. Merry Christmas to all and to all a good night!

January 4, 2001

I had a great Christmas, but I totally got gypped on presents. I did, however get to spend quality time with my family. That is what really counts. It's not the holidays without love.

On New Year's Eve, I went to my friend Katie's house, where we had to clean her room, and my throat was killing me. Then as time kept on creeping closer and closer to midnight, her parents were still downstairs, watching adult movies. We thought for sure we weren't going to get to watch the ball drop. We finally did, though. We celebrated with sparkling grape juice and snacks, and then we watched movies the rest of the night.

The last few days haven't been too eventful. That was until today. I woke up and did my morning routine. I took my meds and sat down to watch TV. Then, as I sat down to eat lunch, my parents tell me I am grounded for a week from every privilege except dogs! What? Dogs shouldn't even have to be a privilege in the first place. They are a part of life, but whatever. Now I'm grounded from the TV, phone, radio, and friends for seven days just because I keep forgetting to do things and supposedly lying about it. I think it is bull, but my parents don't give a rat's ass. I would lose my head if it wasn't attached! They just don't get how I feel and probably never will. All I got left to say now is I hope I live through these next seven days of pure boredom.

January 16, 2001

I am finally ungrounded, and I feel like a free woman again! I swear I am never ever going to tell another lie again, if it keeps me out of trouble. Maybe a couple of small ones here and there, but not big ones! No way!

Here, lately, I haven't been feeling too hot. I have a sinus infection along with a double ear infection. To top that off, my mom keeps bugging the piss out of me to do what seems like every chore she can find for me to do in the house. The way she does it just pisses me off more. She bitches non-stop! I wish she would write me a list, but she refuses, and when I tell her I am feeling like crap, she just tells me to suck it up and do the best I can. Yet, when she feels crappy, she's allowed to bitch everybody around like we are her slaves!

Onto better things now! My brother Philip and I get out of school at 11:00 a.m. on Thursday and Friday this week! Yay! Half days!

Last but not least, I had the weirdest dream last night. Katie was at my cousin Michelle's house. I was at Gamma and Gampa's old house in Fowler, which is only six miles from there. When I went over to Michelle's house, Michelle and Katie were in the basement, playing ping pong with their roller blades on. Then we all went upstairs and her cats started talking to us. That was when my alarm went off. I woke up thinking, wow!

Not much else on this end.

February 2, 2001

Today is Friday. It is Groundhog Day and, yes, Phil did see his shadow today which means six more weeks of winter! This also marks one year since I went to the hospital for suicide attempt and thoughts. What a difference a year makes! I feel great now!

In general, this week has been pretty good except for the fact that I've been sick again and had to miss school Tuesday and Wednesday. I have, however, made up all of my work so I don't have to do it this weekend.

Last Saturday, I went to a cheer clinic at Central High School with the Bearcat cheerleaders. I got a free Tshirt and my mom bought me a set of pom-poms that are now hanging on my dresser mirror. As a part of the clinic, all the girls that participated got to cheer at the Central basketball game that night! I was so proud to be in the spotlight for once!

We had another Titan pride drawing at school. Those are reward cards that we get when we are good. As usual, even though I have a million in there, I didn't win anything. I have bad luck I guess. One of the boys I have a crush on won a razor scooter. I was so pissed, but I didn't let it ruin my day.

I am feeling very calm right now because I am writing my feelings down in a safe place. I'm in my room with the door shut.

Well, I've got to go get some other things done now.

February 12, 2001

I am feeling super depressed again. Every stinking time I get pissed, I have nowhere to put it, so it turns into depression. I don't know how to handle it anymore. My daddy called my guidance counselor a week ago, but she still hasn't got back with me.

My mom is still driving me insane! She has to have everything just perfect. When I am doing my chores, she always tells me that it's not good enough and to do it again. She never gives me enough credit.

Well, for her 411, I am doing the best I can. If she doesn't like it, she can kiss my ass in Macy's window! She makes me so frustrated sometimes that I feel like punching a hole in the wall or just plain go crazy for that matter!

I swear it's like World War III when Daddy goes to work! I wish his freaking supervisors would understand about family!

Instead they sit on their asses while the other employees work theirs off for little pay and horrible insurance! The stupid bastards need to put Daddy back on days like he was for a long time.

He is the negotiator between my mom and me, and, as you can already tell, I'm a daddy's girl, so if u don't like it, go away!

I also miss him being home to help me with my homework, eating dinner with us, hanging out with me when we have free time and my friends are busy or grounded, and tucking me into bed!

I am stuck with my mom basically from the time I walk in the door until the time I go to bed, and there's nothing I can do about it. That's what pisses me off the most! My anger builds up so bad sometimes that I want to hurt her. I know that is not good. I don't want to kill my mom! I have got to get help, but I don't know how.

The psychologist I am currently seeing is not helping at all. He doesn't seem to know when to take things serious. He is always joking about everything.

Well, I've got to go now! Good-bye!

February 15, 2001

I'm still depressed and don't know how to cope. Mom just keeps making it worse. I haven't been doing much of anything.

My guidance counselor finally got back with me today. We talked, and I feel like I might need to be admitted to the hospital for a few days again, at least until I get some meds or something straightened out. I cannot keep feeling this way! I don't want to hurt myself or other people!

In other news, as I was lying in bed, last Tuesday night, I heard a noise. I thought it was my mom in the bathroom, putting something in the cabinet and dropping it. Then when I woke up on Wednesday morning, I got the play by play of what really happened.

Philip was on the computer and saw a flash from out of the corner of his eye, then heard a big explosion. My mom had heard it too and came running outside to see what all the commotion was about. By that time, the fire trucks were coming.

It ended up that the neighbor down the street had just got back from filling up his truck with gas. He had just parked it ten minutes before. He and his wife were just sitting there in the living room, and all of a sudden they heard a loud roar and smelled stuff burning. I guess they just have to thank their blessings that they weren't in the garage because they would have been badly burned or even killed!

February 22, 2001

My mom and I got into it again today! My work is never good enough for her. I could do it ten times over and she would still find something wrong with it! She is the biggest perfectionist I have ever met. None of my friends have mothers that do that.

Hell, most of my friends only have to do one chore and they are done.

She is totally different when it comes to my brother. He is assigned either dogs or dishes, and that's all he's required to do every day. He never gets the chores piled up on him and never gets told that it's done wrong!

I don't know what my mom's problem is with me! She expects me to be just like Philip. She expects me to get good grades and have no problems getting my homework done and have no problems doing my chores.

I am a far cry from him! I wish she would realize that. We are two different people, and we have two different personalities. I guess she's used to a family all the same. That's her family for you!

March 5, 2001

My mom and I are finally starting to get along. Well, for now anyway. She still bugs me here and there, but she is, for the most part, backing down and letting me have a life. I don't know what has gotten into her to make her change like this, but I like it. It's peaceful for once. My friends and I can actually have fun when they stay the night. When she is bitchy, she annoys us all.

In other good news, I saw my first shooting star tonight when I was out feeding the dogs. Duh, of course, I made a wish; now to see if it comes true?

School is going OK now. I do, however, need to keep on studying. It does, however, make me happy to know that I have good grades in all my classes for the first time in ages.

They finally have me in the right group. For the longest time, the stupid school kept on saying that I was too smart for special education. I kept on falling farther and farther behind until finally when I got halfway through last year and I went into the hospital twice. That's when somebody realized that it was about time to do something. It just makes me furious that they waited so stinking long! I had emotional issues, and nobody recognized them. I should have been in these classes a long time before. I was made fun of a lot in elementary because I was way behind emotionally. Now I'm finally in a group that I am comfortable with.

My daddy's birthday is next Sunday. I haven't the slightest clue what to get him or what to do that day. Maybe I can make him something? I will figure it out, I guess!

Well, I've got to go to bed. I'm getting sleepy.

March 16, 2001

Today is a very happy day for me. For no. 1 it's Friday. For no. 2 Grandma Karla is here. For no. 3, she is staying the whole weekend! We are celebrating her birthday late, so tonight we are going out to eat somewhere.

The greatest thing about her being around is when she helps me out with my chores. It's nice every once in a while.

The bad thing about that though is when she cleans my room she puts things away where I can't find them. Sometimes, my stuff goes missing for months at a time. That's why I have to be there to help, so I can show her where everything goes!

March 20, 2001

Well, the sanity at home didn't last long. My mom is back to her old bitchy self again! Sometimes, I think my mom does things just to piss me off.

It's so frustrating as well because she can't hear what I am saying half the time anyway. She is legally deaf. We talk most of the time, though, because she reads lips and has hearing aids, but she sometimes uses those hearing aids to her advantage. If she doesn't want to listen to somebody anymore, she just turns it off. That's just her excuse to avoid her problems.

I'm sorry, but the world doesn't work that way! Just think if all of us did that. You think the world is hell now? There would really be another world war if we all bottled our feelings up!

I can't wait until Sunday. I get to go to Gampa and Gamma's house in Lafayette. That's one hundred miles away from her ass for five days.

Chapter Two
Spring 2001

March 31, 2001

I am so pissed at the world right now. I don't know what to think anymore. My mom never appreciates what I do whatsoever. It seems like no matter how hard I try I can't do anything right for her.

My friend Ashlee did get to stay the night last night, which is a good thing, but she just had to leave a little while ago. That means, right back to hopelessness, and I don't know why but my daddy doesn't seem to be stepping in hardly at all anymore when my mom starts bitching. That just adds fuel to the fire!

I did have a great time at Gampa and Gamma's. Sometimes, I wish I lived with them. There's a hell of a lot more structure when I'm up there and even when they come down here to Muncie. I like a little structure. Not strict structure, but just a little, so I can accomplish things. It makes me feel good when I can get things done in an orderly fashion.

Last but not least, my parents have finally broken down and are getting a new heating and cooling system. We haven't had central air since I was three! They never replaced it after being hit by lightning. It will also be nice to have the new furnace in the winter because my bedroom is the coldest room in the house! Hopefully, this does some good!

April 17, 2001

Sorry it has been so long since I last wrote. The heating and cooling system is one of the best things my parents have ever invested in. It did do some good after all.

I have been extremely busy with school, and life at home is still about the same as the last time. My mom is still the most annoying person I have ever met!

The good thing about being busy with school, though, is it has really paid off! I finally have made honor roll for the first time since the second grade! I also got achievement ribbons in four of my classes for bringing up my grade! I haven't felt this good in a long, long time!

Speaking of things that make me feel good, my dog Minnie and I are in 4-H dog obedience. That means in July we get to be in the dog show at the fair! That also means more of an opportunity for me to feel good about myself! I can't wait! I have been watching Philip get awards and trophies all these years! Now it's my turn!

April, 26, 2001

Life is going OK I guess. School is getting harder now, and my grades are starting to slip. It also doesn't help that when I go home at night, my mother has to start in on me. It never fails. The worse thing about it is that my English teacher is starting to get on my last nerve. It's getting to the point where I think about skipping her class. I don't though. If I did, I would feel so guilty that I would rat myself out!

What keeps me motivated is Mitch. He's the guy I have a major crush on. I sit by him every day. I wish I had the guts to ask him if he likes me too and if he would like to go out. He's so hot, with that muscular butt of his! I stare at it when he is up at the pencil sharpener! Then I go up to sharpen mine, just so I can get closer to him!

Onto other things, yesterday was Minnie's first day of obedience training. She did great and got along with the other dogs well. I figured out that she is also going to need a lot of work before July. Minnie definitely has a mind of her own! I hope I have the patience! I might need a little help!

May 25, 2001

Today started out on a good note, but in first period, it went down the crapper! Me being me, with my head up my ass, I lost my gym clothes and had to sit on the bleachers and do nothing for a whole hour. Then after school, I was relaxing because it's Friday, and Mom comes barging in and says let's go! That bitch had no right to do that! I don't care if she is the birthday girl. It still doesn't give her the right to treat me like her slave!

The next thing that really threw me off was when Katie asked her parents if she could stay the night and they told her no. She had to do a ton of chores too! I swear. Our parents must not realize that there are child labor laws out there. They won't let us be kids while we can.

The good thing about the situation, however is she gets to stay tomorrow night. I hope that her parents don't change their minds! Last year she was grounded for five months just because she didn't clean the whole house! That really sucked balls. She was pretty much the only person I associated with from school last year. She knew everything about me.

Chapter Three
Summer 2001

July 23, 2001

Oh my god! Half the summer has gone by and I have been so busy I haven't had a chance to write.

Here's what has been happening; June went by really fast. I went to a bunch of family reunions. In between then I've been busy with my 4-H photography project, which paid off because just this last week I received a blue ribbon on it! I have also been working really hard on getting Minnie ready for the dog show, which is coming up this Saturday. I am thinking she is going to do well. She has made a lot of progress since we first started in April. I might even get to go to the state fair this year. I'm really excited because I have never been!

When I haven't been working on my projects, I've been hanging out with my friends! In fact, I am going with Katie and her family to Kings Island next week. I really can't wait for that! More time away from my mom!

Speaking of, we are still having our problems. She doesn't listen to anybody!

July 30, 2001

I am at Kings Island and loving it! We have been here for two days now and we are going back to the park again tomorrow. I am at the hotel right now, by the way. We have ridden almost all the roller-coasters including the big ones. Son of beast is questionable. It doesn't look safe to me. Katie keeps on bugging me to ride it, and I keep telling her no, but she won't stop. She's starting to annoy me. She wants her way, and she's not going to get it.

The dog show went great! Minnie and I placed third in our division. I am so proud of myself! I actually did it! We got a trophy with a third place ribbon around it.

Later on in the day, Katie and I went to the fair to ride some of the midway rides and play some games. We won a couple of stuffed animals, and the rides were pretty cool too. For some reason on the last day of the fair it always rains, and this year was no exception. It rained for about a half hour. That's when we played the games.

Well, I have to get ready to go to bed now. I have another long funny day ahead!

August 5, 2001

I'm back from Kings Island now and just getting over strep throat. I didn't think I could get it in the summer but OK. It seems like I can't quit getting sick. I stay well for a couple weeks, then something else happens!

Starting tomorrow, I have to go to summer school. Blahhhhh! There goes the rest of my summer out the window. It's only half day, but still! I hate it because I have to start getting up early again, all because they want me to study for the stupid I-Step test. That's the state's way of judging a book by its cover! Not everybody is at the same level. They, however, don't recognize that and make it so everybody has to stress. What has this world come to? It just keeps on becoming more and more advanced! Hell, before long, they will have babies doing math and reading. Where's the fun in that? What happened to childhood? Now schools have all-day kindergarten. Back when I was that age, we only had half day. Come on people, we need a freaking break here! We are just kids! Let us enjoy it while we can!

August 14, 2001

Summer school is almost over, thank God, now to take the test in September and see how I do? It's usually not too good. I suck in math, and English isn't much better either.

The best thing about being in summer school was that a lot of my friends were there. One day, we even got sent home early because we had a storm with eighty mile per hour winds that came through the area so we didn't have any lights. It got so bad at one point that our teacher had to move us into an interior classroom. We all thought we were going to get sucked up into a tornado. Nothing ever touched down, though. We did have a bunch of tree branches everywhere and, of course, the millions of downed power lines.

Tomorrow, my daddy and I are headed to the school to pay my book fees. That also means I get my schedule. I hope I get some good teachers. Last year they had me with good ones so I trust they will do the same this year. I am also going to try my damnedest to get good grades again.

Later on this week, I have an appointment for the eye doctor and also with the orthodontist. I have to get braces again. Joy! Not!

Last but not least, tomorrow is a holy day of obligation. That means we are required to go to church. I wish we didn't have to. A lot of my friends that are Catholic are allowed to skip stuff like that. Unfortunately, my daddy is hard core when it comes to this matter. He thinks if you miss Mass one time, it's a mortal sin and you will have to go to confession immediately!

August 21, 2001

Wow, this summer has gone by like no other. Tomorrow, I start eighth grade! I am so psyched. I don't know if I will be able to sleep tonight. I can't wait to catch up with my old friends and teachers from last year, and I am so ready to meet my new ones! This year I am on the team called the Astronomers. What that means is that the school divides up all the students into three teams; two of them are split, one of them being the Voyagers. That was the one I was on last year. It is sixth and seventh grade. Then the other split team is the Challengers, they are seventh and eighth graders. The rest are all one grade.

The teams are pretty cool because we all get together as a team to go on field trips and watch movies. We also go as a team to get our pictures taken on Picture Day, and we all have the same lunch. That's not until 12:25 p.m. By that time, we were starving!

I got my braces put on last week. It really sucks because one of my wires is poking my cheek. It's really starting to annoy me. If it doesn't stop, I'm going to have to call my orthodontist back so he can fix it!

August 24, 2001

Boy, did I have a crappy day! School went great. That wasn't a problem at all. I come home and throw my stuff down thanking God it's Friday and I made it through another week. I did my after school routine—eat my snack, watch some TV, call a friend or two.

When 5:00 p.m. came around, my friend Ashlee had asked me to stay the night. I asked my mom. She said, "Yes, but first you have to do your chores that you have been putting off all week." Little did I know that she had a list a mile long! For four hours, I slaved away. I swept pretty much every room in the house, cleaned both bathrooms, and had to do a butt load of dishes.

By the time I was done, I was hungry, thirsty, and extremely pissed because it was already nine thirty. I was so glad to get away from that house and get over there to Ashlee's. I feel a lot more relaxed there. When I finally did get there, I was hysterical for the first hour. I talked to her mom as she was fixing dinner. She agreed with me that my parents could be a little harsh sometimes.

August 29, 2001

Here goes another crappy in the record books. This time it started at school. First off, my stupid gym teacher made me and my friend Heather walk the track the whole class just because we forgot our gym clothes. Then in choir I didn't understand something and my teacher yelled at me.

When I got home, my mom had to start in as usual. She bitched at me as soon as I walked in the door. She had a list of a million and one things for me to do again. By the time I got everything all done, I only had a half hour of free time before I had to take my shower and start getting ready for bed, so now

I am hyper and I feel like hitting people for no reason. I am not sleepy yet either and it's already 10:00 p.m.

September 4, 2001

School went great today, but you know how it goes at home. Not so hot. My mom bitched at me as soon as I walked in the door. She had to check the homework hotline because she never believes me when I say I don't have any. She thinks everybody is a liar if you ask me.

Then Katie asked me if I could hang out this evening, so I asked mom. She said, "No, you have to do your chores." That's when I got so pissed that I could have hit her in her face. She makes me so furious. She doesn't seem to understand that I need my freedom. That's when I don't get my excess energy burned off; it just makes things ten times worse. She only let me have a half hour of free time again.

Thank God, I have counseling tomorrow! It couldn't be better timing. I hope he helps me before I rip her head off!

September 20, 2001

School is going smoothly, and life at the homestead is starting to calm down for now. I love all my teachers. I have been really busy.

Here's what's happened since I last wrote. On September 11, four planes were hijacked by terrorists from the Taliban. That's in Afghanistan.

The first plane hit the North Tower of the World Trade Center in New York City, somewhere around 8:45 a.m. Eastern Time, so seven forty-five in Indiana. The second plane hit the South tower shortly after, as the world watched in horror. There was the third plane that hit the pentagon and the last plane to go down was the one that crashed in the middle of a Pennsylvania field. I forgot which plane it was, but one of them was headed straight for the white house. Some of the family members and friends of the passengers on that flight said that they received phone calls just before they crashed. They are being remembered as fallen heroes because they all ganged up on the bad guys and turned the plane around just in time.

As for the twin towers, they are no more. They finally gave out after the fires had burned for a while. When they did cave, there was a big cloud of dust that sent everybody running for their lives. Several thousands of people are still missing, some are presumed dead, and others are just praying for the best.

There are blood banks open all across the country, and there are also memorial services being held in almost every community, including here in Muncie. It was held at the Central High School Stadium last Wednesday night. Let me tell you something. I have never heard such silence during our National Anthem as I did that night.

Where was I when 9/11 happened you ask? I was taking the I-Step test. Our principal didn't bother to tell us until the testing was all done and over with for the day. What really made me upset was the fact that they wouldn't let us watch it on TV. All we knew was New York City looked like a war zone and the Pentagon had been hit.

I was so anxious. We hadn't even been told that all flights in the United States had been grounded for the day. I was afraid that planes were going to fly right over our house and drop bombs on us. When I finally got home, I turned on the TV and was trying to see what all was on. The news was on almost every channel! They kept on replaying the planes hitting the towers. When I first saw it, I was shocked. I started bawling my eyes out. I couldn't stop watching it. This is definitely going down as one of the worst days in American History! All I have to say now is, "God bless USA!"

P.S. There have also been many songs written in honor of this horrible tragedy! I have been listening to the radio nonstop!

Chapter Four
Fall 2001

September 30, 2001

School is still going great. My favorite teacher is Mrs. Fraley. She is the best one I have ever had! Her class is really small so I can finally get the one-on-one time that I have needed all these years.

Right now, I am waiting for my daddy to get off the pot so we can go get Minnie blessed. They have blessing of the animals today at church.

Dang, I am so distracted. I can't think of much else.

October 4, 2001

I am once again losing my mind! My mother just does not stop her crap! I cannot wait until Mrs. Fraley's class tomorrow.

For some reason, she seems to be the only one who knows how to calm me down. She is so easy to talk to, and she understands me. Sometimes, I wish she was my mother!

As I have said before, my daddy is a whole different story when it comes to my overall health and well-being. Unfortunately, as we all know, he is still working nights. That means being stuck with blah, blah, blah, and do this, do that, from the time I walk in to the time I go to bed! I still wish it was like the old days when Daddy was on days, and the latest he got home was 6:30 p.m! Now the latest he gets home is 3:30 a.m., and sometimes, he even has to work Saturdays!

I hate when I don't have control over these sorts of situations! I guess I'm going to have to look at the positives and do what I can do to change it. You know what they say, "When you have lemons, makes lemonade!"

October 12, 2001

Today, the whole eighth-grade class went on a field trip to the Civil War Days in Hartford City. My daddy was a chaperone with a group of six of us, all girls! He was drowning in the estrogen ocean. Six eighth grade girls + one Dad = oh my god, run! I also saw some of my other friends from 4-H. There were a lot of other schools from the area that were there as well.

I had my first choir concert of the year last night. It went very well considering my teacher is a total bitch. Oh yeah! Did

I mention it's Friday? TGIF, or as my daddy says, "Toes go in first."

Life at home is of course not much different. My mom is invading my space bubble. She never knocks before she comes in my room, and she still nib shits through my stuff. It's like she wants to be stuck up my ass 24/7! All I hear every day is nag, nag, nag!

What the hell does this woman want from me? I am trying to do what she is telling me, but she just keeps on adding more and more details. I am one person, and when she keeps on doing this shit, it just makes me more frustrated at myself and then it takes me longer.

October 23, 2001

Help me! I have this empty feeling that won't seem to go away. I feel OK at school, but when I get home, it consumes me. I tried to talk to my mom about it today, but she just told me to shut up and turned off her hearing aid.

That little priss needs to listen to me! It just keeps getting worse, and just between you and I, sometimes, I wish my parents weren't together anymore. That way I could live with my dad and not have to be around her ass so damn much! Unfortunately, that will never happen. They love each other too much, but she's still ruining my life, and I have got to find a way to stop her!

November 5, 2001

Wow, I turn fourteen in just four days! I can't wait. I'm having a party with my friends right on the big day. Thank God, it falls on a Friday. Then on Sunday, my family is celebrating not only mine but also Grandpa Don's, Aunt Susan's and Gamma's birthday. My parents' twenty-third anniversary is also on November 25, so we always do theirs that day too.

In school news, English and social studies are getting really hard. I got Ds in both classes on my last report card. I think it's about time to ask if I can be moved up to Mrs. Fraley's room for them so I can get more help. I want to be able to go on to high school, dang it!

United States figured out the main man who was behind the attacks on 9/11. Osama Bin Laden is wanted dead by America and the soldiers overseas have bombed several hideouts for al-Qaeda leaders.

November 11, 2001

I am now officially fourteen! That means just two more years until I can drive!

Both of the parties went great. The one with my friends was really interesting. We listened to some music, then we got into the balloons, and Ashlee was the first one to hatch the idea to put them in her bra and knock on Philip's door just to annoy him.

We all had fun with that for at least a half hour. We stood by his door and kept on knocking until he finally came out and stopped being a party pooper.

Ashlee, Heather, and Kenya stayed the night after the other guests left. That was pretty cool. We stayed up until 3:00 a.m. just doing what girls do. We painted our nails, ate snacks, did make up, and watched movies. When we woke up in the morning, my daddy made his "to-die-for homemade waffles." After that, we rode bikes for a while but not too long after that my parents said it was time for them to go home because we had to clean house. It wasn't messy but, whatever.

The family party today was great too. My parents actually broke down and got me a CD. That's a first. They usually get me **el cheapo** stuff or crap that never gets used. It's a miracle! They are not so lame anymore! Philip also burned me my first CD on Thursday night. It has a bunch of my old favorite songs on it, and he added a couple of **"Bob and Tom"** tracks that are hilarious! They're so good I can't quit listening to them! Then I have it stuck in my head all day!

The worse thing in my life right now is that I have a really bad UTI. I can't stop peeing. I go every half hour, and when I do, it's only enough for a mouse. What's really bad is that I had a choir clinic at Central this last Tuesday and I had to have a chaperone take me back and forth to the restroom all day long. Then that night at the concert, I went before it started, twice in between when we were off stage, and I thought I wasn't going to make it through the last song, which was oddly the National

Anthem. You would think that would be first, but anyway that was the night that I was so sick I didn't even stay afterward for refreshments and to say hi to my friends. I headed straight home to bed. Not even ten minutes after I got home and into bed, I got up and puked. Wednesday, I took the day off school to just relax. That and I still felt like shit. I am feeling a little better now, but I'm still peeing like crazy.

Speaking of, I've got to go! Nature calls!

November 19, 2001

Gamma Shipman is sixty-eight years young today! She doesn't act her age, and I mean that in a good way. She is always doing something. She never slows down.

My UTI is getting better every day. My regular doctor sent me to the urologist so he could handle things. I saw him for the first time today, and he prescribed me fourteen more days of antibiotics. He also said no pop, tea, or chocolate. I have been trying to do away with pop anyway because that's what got me into this mess in the first place, and tea, I hardly ever drink, but chocolate! Oh my god! **I need my damn chocolate!** Everybody is going to have to watch out for the next two weeks! I am going to be a pain in the butt!

My choir teacher is officially the biggest bitch ever! She made fun of one of my friends today. I want to quit so bad, but my daddy won't let me. Mrs. Fraley is all for it. She thinks it's a great idea. She thinks I need to be able to choose what I want. My daddy on the other hand will only give me and my brother the choice of band, choir or orchestra. No art or anything else.

You would think because he talks about how bad his parents treated him and gave him limited choices he would be a little less harsh, but no, he has to have a bug up his ass.

I still don't have a boyfriend yet, and I know there are guys out there that like me. They are just too shy to come and ask me out. I am sure, if I give it time, something will happen. Maybe I can make the first approach? I will figure something out.

December 4, 2001

I got my progress report today, and I am not doing so well. It seems like no matter how hard I try to do good I am always failing in at least one subject. I try to get one grade up and another one starts slipping. That's why I'm not allowed to do very many extracurricular activities. It makes me feel so singled out, especially when Philip gets all good grades in school hardly having to try. I'm so sick of him getting all the credit. My parents look at him as if he's the perfect child and I am the rebel. Just because I fail doesn't mean I don't try. I put forth a lot of effort. It's very hard for me to concentrate on all my classes at once. I work at my own pace, and most teachers don't like that. There are only a handful of them that have let me. I need more classes that are like that so I can succeed.

I can't wait until Christmas break. I need it badly. I have another long list. I will most likely get most of it this time because last year I got my bunk bed. I don't really consider that a Christmas present, but that just goes back to my parents being cheap. When we were lucky to get just one thing on our lists, they ended up getting us generic stuff that didn't last half as long. Don't even get me started on things with batteries! Oh my god! My daddy threw absolute fit if Grandma Karla or Aunt Teresa got toys that required them. Who could blame them, though? My parents left it up to them to get the cool stuff. All of our friends had the new toys and games, but what did we have? Toys from the stone-age, pretty much. We were lucky to get that sort of stuff unless it was our birthday or Christmas anyway.

December 13, 2001

I have been puking and having the Hershey squirts for the last five days. I feel like crap. I am at the point now where I don't know if this will ever end. I have been to the doctor twice, and he says it's a bad case of the intestinal flu. It's really bad all right! I haven't been this sick since I was nine months old. That's when they had to put me in the hospital because I had a super high fever and I couldn't keep anything down.

In other news, somebody from the United States found a video of Bin Laden bragging and joking about 9/11. He is obviously proud of what he did and for that he needs to suffer a slow and painful death, or at least some torture! My daddy and I were discussing it the other day, and here's what we think should happen when he is captured! First, hang him by his feet off a chopper and dip him into Lake Michigan in the middle of January, then when they pull him out, don't give him any blankets. After that, ship him by school bus to Death Valley, California, and leave him there for a couple of days without food or water. If he's still alive at the end of all that, they need to take him to his final destination of Folsom, so Bubba can have some fun!

Chapter Five
Winter 2001-2002

December 24, 2001

Wow, has it been a year already? A lot has gone down this year. I have learned to appreciate my freedom, love my country for what it stands for, and what it's like to feel like a winner.

Gamma and Gampa are here today and are spending the night this year. Another cool thing is Grandma Karla is also going to be here, so all the family is going to be together on Christmas Day. We are going to Mass tonight, and after that, we are going to go look at the light displays all around the county. We used to do that every year but for some reason, we stopped. I think it's because Gamma and Gampa used to originally come on Christmas Eve.

I would like to take this opportunity to thank the Lord for my family and pray for all the fallen heroes and their families that lost their lives on that beautiful Tuesday morning that was ruined by the heartlessness of terrorists. I also want to pray for the soldiers overseas, fighting for our freedom each and every day.

I am going to sign off with the Pledge of Allegiance:

I pledge allegiance to the flag of the United States
of America,
And to the republic for which it stands,
One nation under God,
Indivisible,
With liberty and justice for all!

God bless America. Merry Christmas to all and to all a good night!

January 10, 2002

It's officially 2002! Dang, the time just keeps on whizzing by. I got a ton for Christmas including my monthly friend. I guess that was a Merry Christmas from Mother Nature. Here's what else I got. I got a Pooh calendar, a Pooh comforter, make-up, a purse, two key chains, a Pooh lamp, and a Pooh T-Shirt. Oops! I almost forgot a frog necklace and some candy.

Today, I had to do and oral report on the digestive system in science. That was an easy A. I worked with a group so I didn't have to take it home. Oh, and Mitch was in my group! If only he knew my feelings for him!

My mom is getting on my nerves again as usual. Not only that but my counselor too. He still doesn't seem to know how to be serious. I'm trying to get the kids to stop making fun of me at school, and the advice he gives me just makes it worse. The stupid comebacks that he has come up with just makes them come up with more names like the r word (retard), Chunky Monkey, Weirdo, Psycho, and a whole bunch of others I can't think of right now. A group of girls also started a rumor that Katie and I were a couple just because we were arm wrestling at lunch. They said that we were holding hands, so now, when either of us is going down the hallway, there are people that shout out the name lesbo. Katie has even had a girl push her up against her locker just to be a bitch!

Sometimes, I wish I had powers to make myself invisible, so that way I could give them a piece of my mind. I would probably scare the shit out of them and make it so they wouldn't mess with me or anybody for that matter ever again!

January 13, 2002

Dear God, help me! I can't sleep! It's almost 10:00 p.m., and I am not the least bit sleepy yet. It's been this way since break, and my parents don't seem to be listening to me. They just give me this herbal supplement that smells like hog poo. That of course doesn't do anything.

This can't keep on happening. It's starting to really affect my brain. I toss and turn every night until at least 12:00 a.m! Then, when my parents go to wake me up in the morning, I am so out of it I am still talking in my sleep. I am also having a hell of a time staying awake in class. That is definitely not good. I am usually very alert. I know I've got to get help soon, or I am going to get really sick.

I have to go. My mom is bitching at me to turn the light off!

January 21, 2002

My parents finally got me an appointment to see a new counselor. Thank God! It's about time. I need somebody who knows when to be serious and to give me good advice on how to fight those bullies off in a good way. I was about to the point where if my parents didn't do something and quick that I was going to take matters into my own hands. Most likely, I would have gotten into a big fight with at least one of the girls that started the rumor. The reason for such drastic measures is because we have been to the principal several times about it, and he did nothing! My parents have even been in there and said something and still not a word to those little snotty ass whores!

My doctor also put me on something to help me sleep. Now I am getting my beauty rest again. You should've seen me when I wasn't on those meds. I looked like the bride of Frankenstein!

January 29, 2002

I just got my first camcorder last week. I've been having so much fun with it. There's always something to catch on film. The day I got it Katrina was with me, and we ran into Ashlee right before we checked out; so right then and there, we asked our moms if it was OK if she stayed the night, and they both said it was OK. When we got back to my house, we fired that thing right up. We played with it half the night; annoying the crap out of my brother running around the house being hyper letting the dogs in and playing with them. Then Ashlee got into the make-up and made it look like she had scratches all over her face. That's when Katrina was hiding, and when I went to go find her she jumped out of nowhere and scared me!

A few days later I took it to Gampa and Gamma's so I could film their fiftieth wedding anniversary party. That one was funny and interesting. Let's just say, when you get my daddy's side of the family together it's big, loud, rowdy, and everybody is there to have a good time. And because the family is so big, when it comes to a funeral, there are some tears, but we celebrate the life so it's just another get together. Sometimes, there's even beer!

February 5, 2002

I finally went to my new counselor today. We talked, and I drew a couple of pictures to help her identify the problems I am having. She is going to have my mom come in every so often to see if we can solve some of our problems and make life a little more calm. Hopefully, it works.

School is going a lot better now. I have worked so hard that I made the 3.0 honor roll again. God bless Mrs. Fraley. She has helped me so much this year. She made it so I have her for four classes now; math, reading, social studies, and science. I wish I had her seventh period. That's when choir is. I need that time to wind down from my day, and if I need help with any of my other subjects, I can get the one-on-one so I don't have to take it home and have hell from my mom! Unfortunately, I still can't get it through my daddy's thick skull to let me.

We had another half day yesterday, and Katrina came over. We started a new video segment we call "Girl Talk." It's pretty much self-explanatory. We basically talk about our personal teenage lives with a little humor.

United States thinks they might have killed Bin Laden when they bombed one of the main hideouts the other day. Not much else.

February 14, 2002

My mom is ruining my life! I haven't got to hang out with my friends in. I don't know how long!

My Valentine's Day was terrible. First of all, my parents yelled at me this morning and sent me out to the bus without a hug or a kiss. Then I started crying on the way to school, and of course, everybody started asking me what was wrong. I stopped crying for a little bit, but then in first period, when I heard the relaxation music in Mrs. Fraley's class, it made me start crying again. Somehow, I managed to get myself together in time for second period, which is English, downstairs. I made it through that class. I, however didn't make it through the third. That's when Mrs. Fraley sent me to my guidance counselor where I finally let it all out.

When I got home and Daddy left for work, my mom immediately started in. After a while of doing chores and homework, she gave me my Valentines gift. I was hoping for something cool, but instead I got a bag of stale gummy bears. Gee, I really feel loved, all right. The only thing I did today that was fun was go to Fazoli's. I guess you can say my life sucks right now.

February 18, 2002

Today has been OK I guess. Both my parents are getting on my nerves now. They argue back and forth all the time, and when they yell and scream at each other, I either go in my room or go outside. Sometimes, they take it out on me for no reason at all. That's when I feel like curling up into a ball in my room and not coming out for a while or just disappearing. They also don't understand that yelling at me makes things a lot worse. I can't get my work done, and when my mom tells me to do things, she usually yells and tells me more than one thing at a time. That really confuses me.

Onto better things now, Aunt Teresa took me to the Castleton Square Mall yesterday for the first time. That's in Indy. I bought a pair of black jeans and a T-shirt that says angel on it. The other good thing is that Ashlee is here staying the night and tomorrow is President's Day, which means there's no school.

Speaking of school, I am failing English again. Grrr! I am trying my best, damn it! The good thing is that my parents don't know yet, so hopefully I can get my grade up before they find out.

February 22, 2002

Today was great! Mrs. Fraley came back from being sick for two days. My mom and I also got to meet her daughter Marcie while we were at the grocery store shopping. That's where she works as a cashier. We are supposed to be getting together sometime soon.

Life at home is the same. My mom is still annoying, and my parents are still arguing, maybe because of the medical bills? My daddy's insurance doesn't pay jack. We don't have dental or visual either and my mom, my daddy, and I all have glasses. Philip is the exception. Luck box!

School is getting harder again, even in Mrs. Fraley's class. Math is getting hard. I suck in long division. It takes me five minutes on one problem. I need a calculator, damn it!

February 23, 2002

Today, I am not a happy camper! My mom has taken over again! She is telling me I can't have any fun whatsoever. She takes my privileges away when I make the tiniest mistakes. When Philip does something like that, he gets a slap on the back of the hand. Why can't I be the star child? I get in trouble for everything. When she saw my progress report today, she said, "I thought you could do better than that!" I keep on telling her what is going on that I don't understand some of the work, but she won't listen. She just starts yelling, and you know what that does to me. That's why I'm afraid to come to her with my homework. She confuses me, and it always leads to a fight.

I am getting my work done, though. I either do it without her at home, or I wait and have Mrs. Fraley help me with it. I think the reason I'm not doing so well is because we are supposed to be reading a book in English, and because I don't understand it, I haven't been passing the quizzes we have been having.

February 24, 2002

Life is still a struggle, but I am taking it day by day. It's starting to look up in some aspects, I guess.

I'm finally getting to have a life with my friends again. I stayed the night with Katrina last night, which was pretty cool. We played around with the camcorder again. That's when I discovered that Katrina's mom doesn't like to be on camera. We woke up this morning and went to her church at 10:00 a.m.! Then we went over to my house and went to my church at 6:30 p.m.! It's been a long day. I'm getting sleepy now.

February 27, 2002

I finally have plans to hang out with Marcie. She invited me to go cosmic bowling this Saturday night at 11:00 p.m., and then I am staying the night at her house in Albany. That's also where Mrs. Fraley lives. It's going to be a little bit awkward hanging out with her outside school. I can't wait though!

Counseling is working out a lot better now. My mom is actually following along with her advice. Let's just see how long it lasts.

Oh, by the way, Bin Laden is still alive. The coward is believed to still be hiding somewhere on the border of Afghanistan and Pakistan. I think it's sad how he made everybody think he was dead and then came out with another video saying, "Try and catch me now!"

I'm getting sleepy. Nighty-night sleep tight. Don't let the ass crabs bite!

March 9, 2002

Today was cool. Katrina spent the night last night and just left a little while ago. That was right before the lights went out. It's really windy outside, and according to the radio, at least ten utility poles have snapped and they don't know what time they will be able to restore all power. I'm so bored right now. I'm not sure what to do after I get done writing. It's already dark outside, so I can't go out and walk. The boogie man might get me. I hope the radio lasts all night; that way, I don't lose my mind. I also have a ton of crayons and coloring books that can keep me busy, I guess.

Onto other things, I ended up not getting to hang out with Marcie last weekend. I was sick. We are supposed to make it up sometime, but I'm not sure when because she is always so busy between school and work. She is getting ready to graduate in May.

March 18, 2002

Today was slow but interesting. Weird things started happening even before the bell rang this morning. It all started at breakfast when a girl's mom came running in and started bitching at her. That definitely doesn't happen every day. Then every time I turned around, somebody was puking on the floor. I guess the stomach flu is going around really bad right now.

After school, I had a doctor's appointment. He said he wanted to test my blood for diabetes and told me to come back tomorrow morning. Mom, however insists we wait until next week when I'm on spring break, so I don't miss anymore school. I am so anxious! I don't know if I can hang on for that long. She of course doesn't understand.

Chapter Six

Spring 2002

March 28, 2002

It's finally spring break, but I have been so busy that half the week is over and I haven't had a chance to write.

Here's the scoop on what's been going on. Sunday night, after my family celebrated the March birthdays at Grandma Karla's, I went home to Gampa and Gamma's. On Monday morning, we woke up to find four inches of snow on the ground. That was the day we had to go get Michelle in Terre Haute. What usually is a two-hour drive was three and a half because the roads hadn't been plowed yet. Fortunately, they were on the way back.

Tuesday morning, we woke up to find that it had snowed even more. It was now a foot. Gamma gave me the choice of either going sledding or going to the roller rink. I ended up going skating. When I got back from doing that, I challenged Michelle and her boyfriend to a snowball fight! We played out there about two hours, just throwing snowballs, making snow angels, and wrestling. That was until Gamma called us in for dinner which was her famous goulash.

By Wednesday, some of the snow was melting. Gampa got up early, like he always does, and got doughnuts for breakfast. Michelle and I played a few rounds of Mouse Trap. I got bored with that and started coloring, and then we went to eat at the restaurant called Roly Polye's. They have sandwich wraps that will knock your socks off! You can put whatever you want on them. After that, Michelle had to work on her 4-H ceramic project, so she took me with her. I painted a cute little dog.

This morning we woke up, everybody else ate breakfast, and we all headed back to Muncie, so I could get my blood test done. When that was all over we met my parents and Philip at Subway. I was so hungry that I could eat a horse.

Now I'm back at home, anxiously waiting for school to start back up. I am so bored.

March 30, 2002

My life is officially a living hell once again! I feel like there is nothing left to do! I don't know what to think anymore!

I got my stuff to sign up for high school the other day, and of course, I asked my parents if I could take art. As soon as the word came out of my mouth, my daddy said, "You have to take either band or choir! Anything else is out of the question!" He still won't let me make the decision for myself. How does he expect me to grow up when he keeps pulling this crap?

I need a punching bag so bad right now; it isn't funny! It pisses me off so bad that nobody, not even my teachers, can get it through his thick skull! He doesn't seem to understand that I don't know how to read music! I have told him several times. He is too set in his ways!

April 2, 2002

Life is good, but I am still being forced to take some form of music. Today is Thursday, and it's nice out for once. Tomorrow, Katrina is coming over to stay the night. Hopefully, Daddy lets her stay Saturday too. We always have so much fun. It's supposed to be nice all weekend.

April 8, 2002

Everything is getting harder again. I am starting to have doubts as to whether or not I'm going to graduate. I'm also praying that I can learn to control my sailor mouth and not lash out at people for no reason. It seems like since I learned all those dirty phrases when I was young, I just can't stop myself, especially when I get mad. I have been praying like crazy for God to guide me in the right direction, and I am trying my best to watch my language.

April 22, 2002

Things just keep on getting better for me. I finally have a boyfriend. The other good thing is that Daddy is on a new work-training schedule. That puts him working 12:00-9:00 p.m. until further notice.

I now have more confidence that all will be OK, that I will make it, and hey, I just noticed no bad words!

Oh my goodness, God is officially leading the way! He is the man! You've just got to have faith! I am growing closer to him every day, and it feels great! I now feel at peace with everybody and everything. Thank you, and God bless!

April 24, 2002

Today was another half day of school, and just like the last couple, Katrina rode the bus home with me. We went on a long bike ride, and we just took her home a little while ago because Minnie and I have practice for 4-H tonight.

On the subject of the dog, she is doing very well again this year. She isn't the best, but not the worst. I'm hoping we do better than last year. We had a prissy little Yorkshire that took Grand

Champion, and I want to show her that mutts are just as good as pure breeds!

May 13, 2002

School has been going really fast lately. It seems like just yesterday it was August. We have eighteen days until we get out for summer.

Mom is going back to her old ways again! She follows what the counselor says for a little while, but then she hates the routine and wants to do it her way. That's why we don't get along; she is not willing to change.

My counselor and I have come to the conclusion that I am going to have to learn some coping techniques to live with her behavior. I can't change her but I can sure as hell change me!

May 15, 2002

There are sixteen days left until summer break. There is so much going on right now that I am so confused. I feel like I am losing my mind. Sometimes, I just want to curl up in a ball and stay for a couple days until this feeling goes away, but I know that won't solve anything.

Since it's been nice lately, I have been either rollerblading or riding my bike to try to eliminate the excess energy that I have. That helps a lot. I sometimes color too. That's usually at night though.

May 31, 2002

It's now officially summer break! I can't believe that I am going to be a freshman in the fall! What really makes it the real deal is that we had an eighth grade graduation ceremony! The sad thing though is that I'm going to really miss Mrs. Fraley.

Monday, the whole Astronomers team is going on a class trip to Kings Island. What's really cool is we're going on a tour bus with TVs and stuff. Sierra gets to go too, so we are going to be buddies for the day. I am so excited!

Chapter Seven
Summer 2002

June 22, 2002

My summer is going great. Obviously, you can tell. I have been so busy that I haven't gotten a chance to write in three weeks.

Kings Island was a blast. Sierra, however isn't a coaster queen like me, and I didn't want to ride alone, so we rode the easier rides. We also played games and won a ton of stuffed animals. I think that was actually the most fun part of the trip. We didn't get home until 11:30 p.m! Sierra fell asleep on the way back. Me on the other hand, I was wide awake and watched Shrek.

June 28, 2002

My parents, brother and I are leaving for Washington DC on Monday, and of course, I am going to write while I'm there so you can hear all about it. We are going for vacation but also because my mom has a (NAD) National Association of The Deaf Conference. I'm really looking forward to this because this is my first time I have been to the nation's capital!

Today is Friday by the way. Ashlee is here, and it's almost 1:00 a.m. My daddy should be home any minute. That's OK we're about to go to bed. We have already taken our pills, and we are watching a movie.

Speaking of family, the Shipmans got together for the annual summer activity last Wednesday. We went to Turkey Run State Park this year and I rode a horse for the first time since I was little. In fact, we all rode horses except for Gamma and Nut Nut (Aunt Annette). We went swimming after that because it was really hot. Then we finished off the day with dinner at the inn and headed back home which took two and a half hours.

July 3, 2002

We've been in DC for two days now, and we have done a lot so far. We got here Monday at about 6:00 p.m. after twelve hours in the car with stops of course. When we finally got to the motel, we thought it had a pool, but just our luck, "nope!" That's what you get when your parents get a cheap hotel! Then my parents made us walk seven blocks to the restaurant, and my legs were stiffer than a deer that's been dead on the side of the road for three days. I was not a happy camper. I was hot, irritated, and wanted a pool, damn it! Then there was the fact that I had to share a portable CD player with Philip the whole way there because I totally forgot mine. I just wanted to scream!

Tuesday morning, we woke up to get our continental breakfast and come to find out they have no tables or anything, so we had to take trays back to our room, which was downstairs. I almost spilled cereal and milk all over me because I'm so graceful.

Thank God, we are checking into the Marriot tomorrow for Mom's conference. We know they have a pool and a continental breakfast there. In fact, I have been told there are two pools.

We have been sightseeing for the last couple of days, and it has been extremely hot. Tomorrow, the high is supposed to be ninety-nine with a heat index of 110-115! I hate it that my daddy is making us go out in it. I wish he would just let us swim until the fireworks. That's when my mom is going with us to the monument.

It's very interesting around here with it being the fourth after 9/11. Security is definitely tight around here. There are choppers everywhere. The white house is even fenced off now so nobody can tour it; I guess because of the security risk. That really sucks because that is usually the highlight of your experience here. Damn terrorists!

July 24, 2002

Wow, three weeks to go until I start high school! Where did the summer go? The best thing is, no summer school!

It's already time for the fair, and the dog show is Saturday. I am so nervous because Minnie has such a short attention span compared to all the other dogs in our division. Now all there is left to do is work with her the best I can and see how she does.

Enough on that subject, and onto the positives! With it being summer, I have been hanging out with my friends pretty much every day. Heather moved back about a week ago, so we are catching up on the time we lost. I have also been hanging out with Katrina almost every day. We switch between our houses because she has a pool. In fact, that's where I'm going here in a few minutes. Marcie has been so busy that we have only hung out once and Katie and I have twice.

July 28, 2002

The dog show was not good. Minnie did not cooperate at all. When I called her to come, she ran to my mom and we ended up last. We did, however, get a grand champion in showmanship, but that was because we were the only ones in our division. I didn't feel like we earned that one fair because there was no competition. My arts and crafts project got a blue ribbon, thank God, but I am still shooting for an honors. For once I want to know what it feels like to be on top. I have always been just an average everyday person that nobody notices.

In other news, I finally got my braces off last week, so I'm getting my retainers. Then on August 9 I have to have surgery on my foot, and I will have to rest it for a few days. It sucks! You know how active I am!

August 19, 2002

School starts on Wednesday, and to get us ready for it, we had freshman orientation last Friday. Sierra was there, which was cool since I haven't seen her all summer. I also saw a bunch of my old friends, and I met some new people as well, but for some reason, when I'm in a big group, I just stick with the ones I'm the closest to.

Sierra and I stayed together the whole day as we played games, ate lunch, and got into a Congo line where I got my foot stepped on. That obviously didn't feel too good, but me being tough like I am, I just sucked it up and went on.

After it was over we asked our parents if she could stay the night and the answer was yes. We made a video and trash talked a few people. Then we had to go pick up Philip from work where we got free ice cream. When we woke up Saturday, we went swimming with Kenya, and I was hoping she would stay another night, but she didn't want to.

August 27, 2002

We've been in school now for a week, and it's going pretty good. There is one thing that gets me though. None of the teachers will write hall passes to go to the restroom. They expect us to go during passing period, which is five minutes, or at lunch. What they don't seem to realize is the fact that the ladies room always has a line no matter what, and it doesn't matter where you are, when the bell rings, we are marked tardy. If we have to do number two or take care of other lady business, it takes even longer and we get the chance of being written up. If they are going to throw such a bitch fit about it, they either need to make the bathrooms bigger or make the passing period longer.

Everything else is great. Lunch is five minutes longer and they have more food choices. They even have a salad/baked potato line. I like all my teachers but Ms. Linda. It's only the first week, and she's already treating me like I'm stupid. My resource teacher has three guinea pigs. I got to hold one today, and he started nibbling on my fingers. I guess they tasted good since that class is right after lunch.

In non-school news, my mom brought up the suggestion that I'm old enough to get contacts. My daddy on the other hand is being a cheapskate and says if I want them I will have to pay for them on my own. I wish he wasn't so old school. Sometimes, my mom goes behind his back and does things anyway so we can have a life. I hope we can do that one day while he's at work. I'm sick of wearing glasses all the time. It's time for a change!

September 16, 2002

School is still going OK. Unfortunately, they changed my schedule and my teacher of record to Ms. Linda and now I have her for three classes.

I am single once again. My boyfriend of four months broke up with me the second day of school. I just forgot to mention it. Although, think it was a blessing in disguise because he is doing drugs.

Speaking of relationships, my brother is now engaged to his longtime girlfriend Joe, who also happens to be Katrina's sister. Philip wasn't the first one to tell us either. It was Katrina. He's always so secretive about everything.

I still can't believe that five days ago marked the first anniversary of 9/11! It seems like just yesterday.

Chapter Eight
Fall 2002

October 1, 2002

I have another boyfriend now, but I still have feelings of emptiness. Maybe it's because I am starting to struggle again at school. They don't have me in the right classes. I am classified as emotional handicapped and come to find out my school doesn't even have those classes at all. I need what I had last year in Mrs. Fraley's class. I had my own cubical, a really small class, behavioral intervention when I needed it, a lot of help to keep up with my assignments and make good grades, and free time after so many assignments were completed. Well, you knew most of that; I was just refreshing your memory, but anyway.

They have me in two classes that are way too damn big. My English class being one where there're over thirty kids. Then there's the class the state just started requiring freshman to take this year called career info and study skills, and there're twenty-five in there. The dumb asses put me in a regular class for that one, so they are going too fast for me. I don't understand any of the work, and the other kids are making fun of me. As you can guess, that is one of the classes I'm failing right now.

I have tried to talk to Ms. Linda about changing my classes to non-diploma track, but she just tells me I need to give it more effort. Whatever I have been and the more I try, the more emotionally drained I become. Sometimes, it's enough to make me want to hurt people, especially her!

October 8, 2002

The countdown is on! Thirty-one days until my birthday! I'm so happy because fifteen means; I'm old enough to get my permit!

I've been living life lately. My parents and I went to October Fest at church last Saturday night. I played some games and won some Mardi Gras beads, made some spin art, and sang Karaoke with my daddy. That's also the night I got a surprise. Mitch came with his mom and step-dad, so we hung out for a little bit. I showed him the inside of the new remodeled church, and he was amazed.

I still wish we could get together. I am single and looking again by the way!

October 21, 2002

Ten days until Halloween, nineteen days until my birthday! My mom says I can't dress up this year and go trick-or-treating because I'm too old. What does she know? I know people who are in their twenties that still go. She's such a party pooper!

Dang it! I lost my train of thought. I'm getting too sleepy!

November 4, 2002

Today is Ashlee's birthday. That means five more days until mine! She had a party like she does every year but my mom wouldn't let me stay very long because she's unreasonable and won't let me have any fun. It's a school night, so I had to come home and get ready for bed.

Mom says she's going to sign me up for driver's education in the spring so I will be driving by summer break, with adult supervision of course.

My daddy says I can't get my own car until I'm eighteen, and if I get one when I'm still in school, I can't drive it there. I still have to ride the bus! What kind of bullshit is that? It makes no sense whatsoever! He's going to make us pay for our own car out of our hard-earned money. Then tell us what we can do with it? That isn't going to happen, my friend. My car my rules! I can make my own damn decisions when I'm eighteen, not him! He wants me to grow up and then pulls this shit!

November 20, 2002

I'm officially fifteen! How was my birthday you ask? It was pretty good except for Katrina not getting to come to the November birthday celebration at my house because her sister wouldn't wait five more minutes for her to get home from church!

Life at school lately has been a nervous wreck! Ms. Linda is by far the worst teacher I have ever had! She is very impatient and thinks everybody should already know the things she is teaching us. I hate the fact that she has control over my whole schedule, because every time I try to talk to her about changing it, she gives me the bullshit excuse that I'm not trying hard enough. Well, guess what? Like I said before, I have been doing my best. Trying to learn and put up with her shitty ass attitude all day is not easy either. It pisses me off the way she makes us all look stupid, when one of us has a simple question, because we don't understand something.

I have talked to my parents about her but they don't listen. They just take her side. She is making them think I am slacking by failing me. If only they could take my place for a couple of days, then they would see how evil the woman is!

December 10, 2002

Christmas is again coming upon in just fifteen days! Time just goes by way too fast!

Here's what has been happening since I last wrote. A couple of weeks ago, there were two Asian boys who were fed up with being racially harassed by another student, so one of them decided to grab a hammer and rearrange the guys face with the claws. They succeeded, all right. The guy almost lost an ear, but he is back to school again. As for the two other guys, they are locked up and facing charges of attempted murder and assault with a deadly weapon. The saddest thing about it was that there were innocent bystanders that got hurt that day, too, as pretty much the whole student body watched one of the nastiest fights in school history.

Onto better things, I had to start going to another counselor today because, as you know, my daddy's insurance doesn't pay for shit! I like this one a lot too. She is even into one of my favorite shows!

Chapter Nine
Winter 2002-2003

Merry Christmas! *Feliz Navidad!* We have a white Christmas! We got eleven inches of snow last night. The craziest thing is, Grandma Karla was at my uncle's house in Portland and she decided to go ahead and come. What usually takes thirty minutes took three hours. She had to go ten miles an hour the whole way. Thank God, the plow was right in front of her most of the time because she probably wouldn't have made it. After she got here all safe and sound, my parents insisted we had to go to midnight Mass, even though we couldn't see ten feet in front of us. When we went, the snow was up to the toes of our boots. When we got out about an hour later, it was up to our ankles! Yah, my daddy isn't a hard core Catholic or anything. That's why he made his family go to church in the middle of a big-ass snowstorm when there's nobody else on the road! You also know that when Gampa and Gamma cancel on us it's really bad! If the weather cooperates, they will be here on New Year's Eve.

This morning when we woke up, I went out to see the dogs, and it's now up to my shins! I just challenged my brother to a snowball fight a little while ago. I won!

Here in a few, Philip and I are going to Katrina and Joe's house to hang out. Katrina is going to show me what all she got for Christmas. She always gets a little more because her parents are smart and start shopping at the first of the year. Not to say that I got gypped this year because I got a lot. Surprisingly, I got most of the things on my list for the second year in a row!

January 3, 2003

Now it's 2003! Time is going fast. That means break is almost over and school is starting back up soon. That also means going back to the hellhole I call Ms. Linda's class! I'm going to miss the peacefulness that I have felt these last two weeks I have been away from her crazy ass. I do miss my friends and other teachers though. That is one of the good things that make me look forward to going every day.

Right now, I'm at Gampa and Gamma's, trying to make the most of the time I have left of my freedom. Unfortunately, this is the last night I am here. Tomorrow morning, they are taking me back home. I'm not sure what to do after that. Maybe my parents will let me have a friend over to stay the night and we can go sledding. I know one thing; I cannot be bored. It makes me depressed!

January 14, 2003

Today was freaky! First thing this morning, Katie came up to me at my locker and said she needed to talk to me. I said, "OK, shoot!" Then came the words that I never expected. "My mom is pregnant!" Wow, I was in shock. She said that her parents had been hiding it from her for a couple of weeks because they weren't sure how she would react. I don't know why they were so worried. She was really excited!

Then tonight, when I was at Heather's, she gave me a cigarette. I smoked it, then smoked three more. Damn, they were good. It helped to relieve the stress that I have been going through lately. I know one thing I'm doing when I go over there now.

January 21, 2003

Katie's mom sadly had a miscarriage. She was only six weeks along, but nevertheless it was still a living being. I am really too sad to talk about it anymore.

Onto other things, Heather is going to Southside now because she lives in that district and the school system is being gay. They say she has to go there even though she's right on the dividing line. That means we don't get to see each other that often anymore. What really sucks is her mom makes her do chores all the time, and half the time, even when she gets them done, she's not allowed to hang out anyway.

January 29, 2003

Today was the day my mom had to go to court over my brother's dog, Jake. I forgot to mention it, but in December the dogs got out. Heather and I chased them a block until I caught Minnie. As we were still trying to get ahold of Jake, there was a lady that was coming out to offer a hand. When she opened the door her little dog followed her barking, like a normal dog does. Jake saw him and immediately charged and went for his neck. That's when he took off and carried the poor helpless dog all the way back to our front yard. My mom was already standing on the front porch, wondering if we needed help, and saw what she thought was a rabbit. When she walked over she then realized it was a little dog, so she shook Jake's collar hard until he let go.

The good news is that the other dog did survive. They said his whole trachea was dislocated, but they were able to fix it. He had to be fed by hand for the first seventy-two hours.

It was ordered by animal control that Jake had to stay in the pen for ten days after the incident, and if the other dog would have died, Jake would have had to be put down immediately. We are also required by the court to pay all the vet bills in full.

I don't know how many times I have told Philip that he needs to work with his dog more. He just tells me that we don't have the patience and that he is well trained. In reality, the dog has no manners whatsoever or we wouldn't be having this problem. Minnie on the other hand is great. She may not be dog-show material, but she knows how to listen to commands.

In other news, Mom and I are getting along much better again. My daddy is working four days again, which keeps the peace, but it's a bad thing when it comes to money.

February 6, 2003

Life is still going great at home, and it's pretty good at school except for those three classes. You know the story, so I'm not even going to go there.

I signed up for 4-H again today. I can't believe this will be my third year already! This year I'm taking scrapbooking, arts and crafts, and the usual dog obedience. The fun thing about it is that I have never done a scrapbook in my whole life, so I'm about to learn something new. It's about time because I have tons of pictures just piling up and nowhere to put them.

Valentine's Day is almost here as you know. It's too bad I will be at a youth retreat all next weekend because a boy asked me to the sweetheart dance Saturday night. It's all good though. I am going to this thing for a reason. I believe that God has called me. I am hoping to get closer to him and possibly make some new friends.

Heather's mom is finally starting to let her off her leash! She's actually letting me stay the night tomorrow night. Before that, I have to help serve spaghetti for the church's annual spaghetti dinner and auction to help support our sister parish in Haiti.

February 18, 2003

Snow, snow, snow! I wish it would go away! We haven't seen the ground since the beginning of December. We had another storm that dropped fourteen inches and then started blowing and drifting that started last Friday night. I thought the youth retreat was going to be canceled for sure, but it went on as scheduled. It's still bad enough that we had another two-hour delay today.

I had a great time, but as far as sleep goes, I got about six hours in two days. I made some new friends and I did indeed get closer to the Lord. I experienced a new feeling when we did Eucharistic Adoration on Saturday night. I have never felt so free and calm to let it all out. I wish I could do that more often.

Definition for those of you who don't know what Eucharistic Adoration is: The Catholic's way of meditating around the exposed body of Christ.

March 4, 2003

Life isn't going so good anymore. My mom is at it again! From the time I walk in the door from school to the time I go to bed, she is on my ass about something. If I do my chores, she just finds more for me to do and bitches at me if I don't do it to her liking. I can't enjoy myself anymore. She is taking away my privileges again for my smallest mistakes. Well, I didn't do something right again. I've got to go. I'm getting bitched at for the millionth time today!

March 14, 2003

My life is starting to go a lot better now. I guess I was having a bad day the last time I wrote.

Spring break starts in exactly a week! As you can guess today is Friday. All I have to say to that is TGIF! Thank God it's Friday! The snow has finally gone; it's fifty degrees. There's not a cloud in the sky; the birds are singing, and it's pretty quiet except for my neighbor across the street whistling. I'm up in the tree enjoying it all for the time being.

My mom promised me that we would go to the store in a little bit so we could pick out paint for my room. This will be the first time it's been done since we moved in thirteen years ago. I say bye-bye to that boring cream color. I'm looking for something along the lines of light purple! That's my favorite color by the way!

Chapter Ten
Spring 2003

March 26, 2003

This week has been kind of boring for my spring break, but it's about to get a hell of a lot better. I've been at Grandma Karla's house for two days now, and no offense, but there's just not a whole lot to do there.

I am on my way to Gampa and Gamma's now. Grandma has never been to their house even though they have lived there six years. That is changing today because that's who's driving. I can't wait to get there. Gampa and Gamma always have more things for me to do.

April 7, 2003

I once again have a new man. His name is Mike, and it might be too soon to say, but I think he might be the one! He's so nice. I was crying today, and he bought my lunch. I now know what it feels like to be in love.

Katrina stayed the night last Friday, and she twisted my hair. Then on Saturday, we went to the mall and walked around and went to one of those photo booths to do some goofy pictures.

Life at the homestead is going fairly good again. Mom rarely bitches anymore. That's because before daddy goes to work he writes a list of things for me to do and tells her to leave it alone or else the counselor will give her a big long lecture the next time we meet! We have finally found a way to get her to follow along with things. I know it sounds harsh, but drastic times call for drastic measures!

Heather isn't getting to have a life again. Her mom won't let her do shit even though she is doing what she is supposed to. She is pretty much like Cinderella, having to do all the chores, and when it comes to having fun, she's not allowed. It's like her mom frowns upon it.

It really sucks because we haven't been able to hang out in two weeks, and the last time, she couldn't even stay the night. She had to go home and do more housework. I wish we could be together more often. We have so much fun together and we have similar problems so we can relate really well. We give each other advice and share our personal life stories like best friends do. God, I miss her!

April 14, 2003

Today couldn't have been more perfect! It was really warm and sunny out. I rode my bike to Katrina's, and we went fishing at the river. Then when I got home, I played with the dogs for an hour, got filthy dirty like I love to do, and then came in and took a shower. Now I'm winding down, getting ready for bed.

Mike got to come over for the first time last Sunday, after Mass. He only got to stay two hours because he lives in a group home, but beggars can't be choosers. I'm just thankful that he doesn't live on the streets. He got taken away from his family when he was eight years old.

Before I forget again, about a month ago, President Bush declared war with Iraq. We dropped bombs on them within the first couple of days, and there are more and more troops being sent over there as we speak. What I don't get is why we aren't doing this toward Afghanistan? It makes no sense. Aren't we supposed to be looking for Bin Laden?

April 19, 2003

Another awesome day down for the record book! I was outside all day, and it was warm enough to wear shorts again. A couple of my little neighbor buddies came over so we played for a while. I got out the camcorder when they started wrestling and being silly with the cardboard box that they had brought over. Then we ended up in the backyard, playing with the dogs like we always do when they are here. That's also where the sand box is, so we pretended like we were in the movie **Holes**.

While we were doing that, my daddy was finishing up mowing. Then he got a fire going in the fire pit. After a while, he threw some burgers on, and mom got the fries and green beans going. It was my job to set the picnic table. That's one of the chores that don't bug me. At our house, it isn't a cookout without the s'mores! My parents always make sure we are stocked up on marshmallows, Hershey bars, and gram crackers throughout the cookout season. If you're wondering, it's usually April-October.

Katie stayed the night Thursday and went to the Good Friday service with us yesterday. She wasn't too thrilled, just goes along with it because we are friends. After church, we went out and ate fish, because, as Catholics, we don't believe in eating meat on Fridays, during Lent. My daddy said that back in the day it was like that every Friday. That would really kill me because I forget as it is. You see, most of my friends aren't Catholic and don't recognize that kind of thing. I know it's a sacrifice, and I feel like a sinner when I forget.

Speaking of sacrifice, I fasted for thirty hours with my youth group a couple of weeks ago. That was really tough. We went bowling, had a scavenger hunt, visited a nursing home, and then went back to the church to have reflections and finally watch movies. We finally got to eat at 6:00 p.m. It felt so good, but it taught me a lot about what Jesus had to go through for our sins.

Mike gets to come over for Easter dinner tomorrow. He only gets to stay for two hours again, though. This won't be for long though. Pretty soon, he will be able to have all-day home visits when he gets me approved to be on his visit list.

April 22, 2003

Life is great. I always have Mike on my mind, and he calls me three times a day. Wow, I'm so in love!

Easter was fun. He gave me a gorilla that says the phrase "I'm wild about you!" when you press his tummy. I made him an Easter basket with candy and a stuffed lion. Just before he left, we made a music video of us singing our song.

After he left, we had a bad thunderstorm, and it rained the rest of the night. My mom got bored and got out the coupon book to see what there was to do. She found a ticket for a free game of bowling in New Castle. We played four games. My mom kicked my daddy and my asses! That just goes to show that I haven't found my thing yet.

Speaking of finding things, I figured out why everybody is in Iraq. They are looking for Saddam Husain. He has links to al-Qaeda just like Bin Laden, whom of which they are still looking for as well.

May 5, 2003

I am so damn bored! There is nothing to do, nobody to talk to, and it won't stop raining. Nobody is answering their phone! Mike has to call me, because, for some stupid reason, he can't receive incoming calls. Now I'm stuck waiting by the phone, hoping to God he calls soon!

Mike is getting to have more home visit hours with me now. They allowed him to come over both Saturday and Sunday this last weekend.

If you're wondering how that went, we had fun all right! Just before he left on Sunday, he gave me my first hickey. I've been trying to hide it, but unfortunately, when I was in gym class playing tennis today, the wind blew my hair up. My partner noticed and had to shout it to the world! That's how it got around to my resource teacher. When she got wind of it, she took me to the guidance counselor where I got a lecture. She said not to be coming to school with anymore. Well, not that they can see anyway.

May 14, 2003

Why does the school have to be such assholes? They piss me off! They are suspending Mike again for more tardies. Something tells me that Ms. Linda has a part in this. He hasn't had any more, but she likes to pick on certain people just because she can.

Every time he is gone, kids like to push me around. Last time, there were a couple of guys sexually harassing me! The next day, I went to the principal and he did nothing. My daddy already told me that if it happens again he will go up to the school himself and take care of it. They don't want to mess with him. My daddy's got a shotgun, and he knows how to use it!

I have never seen a more sad excuse for a school than ours. For them, to let bullying, sexual harassment, and especially racism go on right in front of their faces. Then they wonder why we have to take matters into our own hands. I also think we have a horrible special education program. The classes are way too big, and there definitely needs to be an emotionally handicapped class for those of us who need it.

May 20, 2003

Wow, it's almost time for summer break again! I forgot to mention this but Philip is a senior so he graduates on the twenty-ninth. It seems like just yesterday we were just kids.

I am watching the news right now, and they just said al-Qaeda might be plotting another attack on U.S. soil. Hopefully, it's just an empty threat. There have been many attempts that have been stopped because of everybody being on guard in this post 9/11 world. The one thing that bugs me the most though is, because of those dumb asses, all middle-eastern people are looked at different. That's like saying all handicapped people are aliens. Let me tell you something. We may be slow, but we are all a far cry from aliens. We are human beings, and my belief is that everybody should be treated equally. I hate when people judge a book by its cover. They take one look and say, "Trash!"

Enough on that subject and onto better things. The Indy 500 is Sunday. That also happens to be my mom's birthday, and I'm not sure what we are doing yet. She will be forty-six.

Monday is Memorial Day and that's when Philip's open house is. Then he of course graduates on Wednesday, and Friday, he turns eighteen! If you lost track, that's on the thirtieth!

As for the underclassmen, we get out on the twenty-eighth. Then Katie, Joe, and I are singing in the choir before the ceremony.

May 26, 2003

Philip's open house was fun! A bunch of people showed up, some of which we haven't seen in a long time. My little cousin was too cute. I wish I would have had a camera handy when he told his dad he had to go potty and his dad told him to go tell mommy, but instead he just peed right there in our front yard! Then Mike got the Super Soakers out and he got me drenched.

After a while, Philip's friend Chris came out and got Mike back for me! Unfortunately, we got bitched at to stop by Gamma. I guess because we were getting the party guests wet when they were trying to visit. That's when we went inside and joined the rest of our gang in playing the Xbox.

In love life news, last Wednesday, when I was visiting Mike, we went up to the dayroom and started watching a movie. The next thing I know we are all alone with no staff, and he tells me to look down. He had his pants unzipped and his thing out. It made me a little uncomfortable. I told him to stop doing shit like that, and he understood.

We finally got our yearbooks the other day. My picture this year is the best one I've ever taken. It was so good that my parents actually bought it for once. Mitch lost his today and came in to Ms. Linda's class, freaking out, swearing silently. Somehow, she heard him, and she wrote him up saying that he cussed her out. That's not true at all. She is a lying bitch that just likes to start drama! God, I can't wait until next year! I know damn well that I'm not going to have her as my teacher of record or for any classes, bottom line!

May 29, 2003

Why does Mike have to live in a group home? The staff treats him like he's five. He's not allowed to live life like a normal seventeen-year-old. They give him stupid curfews of no later than nine, and he can only do stuff on Wednesday nights and on the weekends. Now what really sucks is, just because my mom and I brought him home from school, he's not allowed to go to the graduation ceremony tonight.

I love him so damn much. I will do anything to help him find his family. I think it's sad that he's in the situation he is now. Being a Christian, I feel like he needs a lot of love and one-on-one attention that he hasn't had for years on end. I think God has brought us together for a reason.

June 2, 2003

Summer is finally here! It was the last time I wrote, but I was too busy ranting about Mike.

Philip is hopefully going to be out of the house soon. He has a full-time job, and I think he is looking at them. That means no more leaving the seat up for me to fall in, no more phone calls in the middle of the night asking for him, no more loogies in the bathroom sink, no more hogging the computer and, best and most importantly, I will get more one-on-one time with my parents!

In other great news, my daddy has finally backed down on making me take music. It took the director of special education for the whole school system to get it through his thick skull. She told him straight up that it was wrong not to let me choose, and that it was my choice not his. She is the only one he seems to listen to and take advice from the most when it comes to my case conferences. I'm not sure why that is, but I'm sure glad I mentioned it to her.

I chose 3-D art by the way. I can't wait. I haven't been in an art class since elementary, and I love it so much. It's definitely a hell of a lot better than choir that's for sure, considering I didn't get to advance to the next highest level from last year. It explains a lot. Like I said before, I have tried my damnedest to learn how to read music, but I just don't understand it. I just had to learn the song by listening. Then I had to tone my voice with the other girls, and that was pretty hard too. I'm not saying I'm tone deaf, but when I'm in a large group, it's hard to keep up, especially when the altos are singing different words than the sopranos. Anyway, I'm just glad to be able to go explore new things.

June 11, 2003

This summer so far sucks. It rains every day. My friends are always gone or can't hang out for some reason and, you know, I can't call Mike because of the stupid group home rule that he has to call me.

I guess there're a few good things. I'm finally babysitting. It's pretty fun and the little girl is really easy to handle. We go to the park and swing, and she's so quiet. She doesn't talk much because she's only two, but we do so much. She keeps me busy for sure.

In not so good news, the evil woman failed me in math. That means I probably have to take her class over again next year! Just when I thought I had ditched her she does this shit to me! I swear she is my worst nightmare!

June 19, 2003

The sun is finally shining, and my friends aren't busy anymore. I also finally got contacts because my glasses keep on breaking really easy. Daddy isn't too happy of course, but Mom told him to live with it. She sat him down and said, "Would you rather pay for one pair of contacts and one pair of glasses in a year or pay for three or four pairs of glasses because her glasses are made cheap?" He didn't have much to say after that.

The annual Shipman activity day was last week. We went to Holiday World this year, and we had a great time. I rode the roller coaster called the raven three times, and I bought a picture of my cousin Tina, Daddy, and me on the log ride. It's definitely a keeper.

Mike is doing fine as usual. We met at the mall tonight because his group home was there and walked around forty-five minutes. He's been getting to spend more time at my house on the weekends finally.

Chapter Eleven
Summer 2003

June 23, 2003

Guess what? I bought a pool today. Unfortunately, we can't put it up until next Sunday because Heather's step-dad has to help us. That really bites. Tomorrow, it's supposed to be ninety degrees.

This Saturday is another family reunion. This time it's at Prince's Lakes in Johnson County. Mike will get to come. That is if he gets ahold of his stupid caseworker but that's another different story that we're not going to get into right now. I did take lunch to him today at his work. I was allowed to eat with him so that was pretty cool.

Minnie is doing OK as far as practice goes. She definitely needs a lot more work on healing and recall. She still pulls me every time we walk, and when I call her to come, she doesn't come straight. She walks to the side, and half the time, she doesn't sit. It really gets frustrating when we have been working so hard and all the other dogs are so much more advanced than us. I don't get it! Why is it I have to try twice as hard as everybody else and still come up short? It's not fair and it makes me feel like I'm stupid! For once, I would like to be on top and not feel invisible.

Damn it! The phone just rang, and again, it's for Philip! I am so sick of this shit! Why does he get most of the calls around here?

Oh wait, that goes back to him being the star child. From first places at the pinewood derby four years in a row and three years ending up as a regional champion to four years of cub scout baseball, he has trophies and ribbons out the ass. When I asked my parents if I could join gymnastics, T-ball, or karate, they said no. All because it cost money and my grades weren't good enough!

It makes me furious every time I think back about this stuff. That and the fact that my stupid elementary school had no special education at all, and they were saying that I was too high functioning for those types of classes. Yet they saw that I was having meltdowns constantly, and as soon as I got into third grade, I started to get very overwhelmed with my work. It's sad that the bastards didn't do anything when they saw what was happening, right under their noses! Now they are wondering why I have self-esteem issues!

July 8, 2003

Now I'm at Gampa and Gamma's house, finishing up my scrapbook for 4-H. I chose to finish it here because Gamma is the expert when it comes to this kind of stuff. She's helping me collect the last few pictures and a little more **memorabilia**. The title, if you are wondering, is "Summer Fun."

Somebody is doing an art project in Lafayette with life-size fiberglass pigs. They are scattered all around downtown and down on the levy too. I have taken several pictures, and I also have some brochures explaining the story behind them.

There's also the walkway over the Wabash River. I have taken several photos of the downtown skyline from there. I have also gotten some good ones of the water. With as much rain as we have had so far this summer, it is well above flood stage.

Mike, as far as I know, has been getting along fine this week. He has been calling me here every day.

He is originally from Lafayette. He was born and lived here until he was taken when he was eight. In fact, this is where his case is. That means, every time he has court, he comes up here. Court is usually every four months, just to check up on things. His next one is coming up in six days. He's supposed to be getting emancipated and going into an independent living center that is owned by his group home. He will have a lot more freedom in this setting because staff only checks on him once a day. He will also have his own little apartment.

July 16, 2003

My life is horrible. Mike didn't get emancipated at all! Instead, he was placed in the residential treatment center for supposedly he grabbed the boobs of one of the residents at the group home.

I knew something wasn't right, when I waited by the phone for hours on end. He said he would call me when he got back from court, like he always does. The whole night went by and nothing! I slept on the couch that night, hoping he would somehow call.

Then when I woke up yesterday morning, and still nothing; my mom got on the phone and called the group home. They were actually nice enough to transfer her over to the treatment center where staff let Mike talk to her for five minutes. He explained to her what was going on.

When they got off the phone, she told me the whole thing to me. He's not allowed to talk to me, but he pulled some strings and he can talk to my parents.

I bawled all yesterday morning, and I still have no appetite. I just picture him all alone in that place, and it tears me up inside! I wish he had a family to lean back on. I hate it that he's a ward of the court and that he's been tossed around to three foster homes and numerous facilities, just to keep him from being on the streets.

He says he's supposed to be there until August 20. That unfortunately happens to also be the first day of school.

All I know is that I hope I get to see him again soon, and when I do, I am going to give him the biggest hug and kiss ever! I wish he was in my arms so bad right now. I have never felt this way about anyone before.

As I sit here, writing, the tears are flowing once again. I miss my baby!

July 21, 2003

Things are going a bit smoother than last week, but I still miss him a lot. The good thing about it is that my mom talks to him at least once a day, so I at least know how he's doing, but I would do anything to see his face right now.

In other news, the fair is this week. The dog show is Saturday, and I pray to God that our hard work and determination has paid off. As for my scrapbook, it got a red second place ribbon. I'm not sure what I did wrong. I guess everybody else's was more fancy or something.

July 29, 2003

Today is Mike's seventeenth birthday. I just keep on thinking of him all alone, with nobody to celebrate with, and no cake.

I'm at Gampa and Gamma's again, trying to make time go faster. They help keep my mind off things when I'm here. It sure as hell beats sitting around, watching TV, and looking at the clock every five minutes, praying, "Dear God, just make it August 20 already!"

We still haven't put up the pool. Heather's step-dad made an attempt a couple of weeks ago, but he didn't follow the instructions right, so now we have to wait until my daddy gets around to it. I have a feeling that will be when pigs fly out his ass!

More bad news, Minnie and I got last place again at the dog show. All I can say is we tried. I have come to the conclusion that she is just not dog-show material. She does mind me well, but when it comes to crowds, there's too much distraction. I have decided not to put her through another year of this crap. It's just not for us.

August 9, 2003

I'm feeling much better as the days pass, knowing that there's only eleven days left until I get to see my baby again! I have been meditating a lot. If you are wondering, that's where I throw on a Christian CD, light some candles, burn the incense, and just let all my feelings out to the Lord. It's very relaxing, and it helps me through hard times. I have also written a couple of songs for him, explaining some of the feelings I have been having since he's been gone.

My daddy has finally made it a priority to set the pool up tomorrow! That makes me happier than a pig in shit! Now time will go even faster. I'll be in there all day. I'm a little fishy. The water is my friend!

I'm at Katrina's right now, and she's writing in her journal too. Her dog red is sitting here, trying to headbutt my arm, and it's starting to irritate me. It's between that and every time I go to bend over he likes to try to hump me. I so wish I had a fly swatter!

School registration is next week. That means I get my schedule and see if I have any good teachers. I know one thing; if I see the crazy woman's name at all, I will immediately have it changed. I'm glad she's not my teacher of record again this year. That's a big weight lifted off my shoulders!

August 20, 2003

The first day of school was OK, but my mind was on Mike all day. When I got home, I waited anxiously by the phone as I watched TV to try to keep myself occupied. Finally around 5:00 p.m. came the voice I had been waiting for. It felt so good to let my feelings out to him. I am now back to my crazy redneck woman self! I can't wait until school tomorrow! We will be making up for the time lost. I know I'm going to sleep well tonight!

August 23, 2003

I'm in Paoli with Katrina and Joe at their cabin for the weekend, celebrating Katrina's fifteenth birthday. It's Saturday night, and we just got done eating cake. This morning we left for Spring Mill State Park and stayed there until about 4:00 p.m! We took a sack lunch, walked on one of the trails, and ended up by swimming in their crisp clean pool that had two diving boards!

What's really cool about their cabin is, they have an outhouse, but their dad made it so the toilet flushes. There's also an outdoor shower with wooden fencing around it. It makes me feel like I'm camping again! That's something I love to do!

It sucks that we have to leave at the butt crack of dawn tomorrow. Joe doesn't like to fart around. She's an early person that likes to get things done sooner than later!

September 1, 2003

Today is Labor Day, and it is a total wash out! It rained all day, so much that some of the roads in our neighborhood were flooded, my street being one of them. Katrina and I got so bored that we went out and played in it. We were going to swim in the pool after that, but the water was freezing.

Mike hasn't been able to have any visits yet. That's OK though. He has a job at Wendy's now, so I can go see him there.

We're hoping he can make his second phase soon so he is able to have more freedom.

He's been acting very strange since he came back. He has an attitude, and I wish he would knock it off. It's starting to worry me that it's going to get him in trouble again.

I can't believe September 11 is coming up again. It just doesn't seem like it's been that long. Time just keeps flying faster and faster! Bin Laden is still at large and hiding as usual.

September 16, 2003

Wow, it's been a while since I have written, so here's what's been happening. As of tomorrow, Mike and I will be together seven months. He is also finally on a good streak. When he first came back, he was always getting in trouble. It's been a week so far since his last incident.

The I-Step test started today, but I was home sick. Since he has a half-day schedule and he didn't have to work, Mike came over to check on me. He's not really supposed to but he couldn't help it, since we can't see each other outside of school. I was afraid that his staff would find out somehow, but they never did. He had my mom drop him back off at the school right before it was time for everybody to get out. I'm just glad I got to see him.

September 17, 2003

I'm just sitting here, trying to chill, after taking the math portion of the I-Step test. Can you say stupid, ridiculous, and bogus! Mike doesn't even have to worry about taking it. That lucky bastard! This test is so hard, and no matter how much I try I always fail both the math and English parts.

What really makes no sense is the fact that they have us special education students doing it, and in order to graduate with a high school diploma, we are required to pass the whole thing. Half of us don't even know pre-algebra. How do they expect us to be able to do geometry, regular algebra, and especially probability? I wish the people that make this shit up could take our place and see it through our eyes, and maybe they would see it! Oh wait! This is Indiana we're talking about! They don't do shit anyway. They say they're improving schools, but when somebody asks to see proof, they're not allowed to show it!

Chapter Twelve
Fall 2003

September 30, 2003

This week is homecoming. Today was Twin Day. Mike and I went as twins in American flag T-shirts. Tomorrow is White Tee Day. I have no plain white Tees; mine all have designs on them.

Katrina has a new guy friend. She claims they are just friends, but they are making it seem like it's a lot more than that. I caught them holding hands at October Fest last weekend. I think I also heard something about Sadie's and Prom? I don't know, but I will keep you posted.

Ashlee is being as annoying as ever with her whining. As for Heather we almost never talk anymore because she's still not allowed to have a life.

October 9, 2003

Mike is gone again; this time to a boy school in Kokomo. He was sent the day after I last wrote. Supposedly, he was making sexual gestures toward a female staff this time. Hell sure what to believe anymore.

I still can remember that day perfectly. I got off the bus, and he was waiting for me with tears in his eyes. He explained to me what was going on and that he was going to run. I tried to convince him not to, but what happened from there I don't know. I went straight to my guidance counselor and gave her the scoop. She then immediately called the group home staff, and I believe they tracked him down soon after that.

From what I understand, he is supposed to be there thirty days. I haven't heard anything from him since the day he left. He hasn't even been able to contact my parents this time.

Onto better things, the rest of homecoming week was OK. At least I had that to keep my mind occupied for a bit. Katrina and I went to the game together, then to the dance afterward. She got to stay the night, and when we got back to the house, we went skinny dipping at 11:00 p.m.! That was pretty interesting because it was completely dark and nobody knew!

October 21, 2003

I'm starting to feel lonely again. I've been babysitting all week and that really keeps me busy until they go to bed. Then I'm left sitting here all by myself with my thoughts.

This loneliness has led me to start listening to country music all the time now. I never listen to anything else. I even fall asleep to it. I think I have found who I really am because this tone makes me feel at home and reminds me of my childhood when my daddy used to play it all day!

I miss my baby so bad right now. School is no fun anymore because he has earth science class with me, and when I come in every day to see that empty seat, it tears me up. I wish I knew what he's doing and how he's feeling. We still haven't heard a word. My worst fear is that when his thirty days is done, he won't come back, and I will never get to see him again. All I can do now is pray like hell and hope to God he makes it!

October 30, 2003

My nerves are shot! Mike's thirty days are up on Saturday, and none of us have heard a damn thing. I have been meditating every night, and my friends have been joining in as well. We're all hoping he comes home.

Now to the happy things: Tomorrow, of course, is Halloween. Saturday, I am having a big sweet sixteen party with my friends!

Katrina is staying the weekend, and we are cleaning the house to get ready for the bash! Sunday, my youth group is having a scavenger hunt. Heather, Katrina, and Kenya are going to that.

November 16, 2003

Great news! He's back! He got back November 1, but didn't get all situated until November 3. That's the afternoon I got a surprise call from him. He was at work. The first words out of his mouth were, "What's up, baby? Did you miss me?" At first, I thought I was dreaming, but then I came to reality. I immediately had my mom take me over there so we could talk.

He is back at the residential treatment center but this time, he's allowed off grounds for school and work. I'm not on his phone list yet, which sucks, but I will be soon. He sometimes sneaks and calls me anyway, but that's not very often because he doesn't want to make it obvious. We were going to go to the Sadie's dance together, but his caseworker is a dick and said no.

That brings me to my next subject, Katrina and I went to Sadie's together last night. She taught me how to dirty dance. We danced like there was no tomorrow.

Ashlee came over Friday night, and as I was getting ready to braid her hair, I thought I saw something move. I had Katrina check it and guess what? Leaping dandruff, cooties, lice, whatever you want to call them, she was infested. My mom shit a brick and started bitching. We then caked her hair in gel and took her home.

Right now, we are on our way to Martinsville to see my Great-Grandma Becca in the nursing home. She's not doing too well.

Here in a few, I'm going to have to ask my daddy to stop. I've got to go pee!

November 19, 2003

Life is getting depressing again. I'm happy at school, but when I come home, I feel sad again. I have considered staring myself, taking a bunch of sleeping pills, or doing something to take away this pain. I haven't gotten to go anywhere but school for three days because Ashlee gave me lice. I'm lucky to even be able to get to there. Last time, I missed two weeks. I can't do anything but sit here and let my mom pick at my head. She pulls my hair and then yells at me when she thinks I'm not cooperating. Why do I have to suffer with this crazy woman?

November 29, 2003

Mom is driving me more and more insane! She is the most annoying person I have ever met! I'm so fed up with her shit that I feel like packing my stuff and running. I still can't have anybody stay the night because she says I have to be lice free for two weeks, and it's only been a week and a half. I swear the woman is a germophobic.

Thanksgiving sucked! Mike still can't put me on his visit list, so we didn't get to spend it together. Thank God, he doesn't have to work at Wendy's Monday, because on school days, when he doesn't work, he helps the janitors in the afternoon.

We put up the Christmas decorations today, all except for the outdoor lights. Daddy put them up last Sunday when it was nice.

December 10, 2003

I'm a lot happier now. So much has been happening in my life since I last wrote. There have been bomb threats at least once a week for the last three weeks, and Mike has only been there for one. Luck butt.

I hate it. Every time, we have to evacuate the building into the cold-ass weather. Then go across the parking lot to the field house and wait for the all clear which can take up to an hour and a half. Then by the time we're allowed to go back, our schedule is all screwed up, all because of a couple of dumb asses wanted to get out of class. They end up getting caught and arrested in the end, and then they have a record that haunts them for the rest of their lives.

In other news, I got my feelings hurt today by a kid in my gym class. I thought he was my friend, but when I went to go say "hi," he bit my head off. I almost cried, but I sucked it up and went to my next class where I talked to my friend, and she made me feel a lot better.

Chapter Thirteen

Winter 2003-2004

December 22, 2003

I am so pissed! Mike still can't get ahold of his stupid-ass caseworker! He's been trying for two weeks, and nothing! Now it's too late, and we can't be together for Christmas!

Saddam Hussein has been captured alive. I woke up to hear the good news this morning and listened as I got ready for church. He is now being detained and awaiting trial; now if they could only find Bin Laden!

I am really getting into the holiday spirit, considering the fact that it snowed last night. This makes me want to burn a Christmas CD, so I did. I have some of the classics on there but also some comedy. You know me I can't keep it too dry!

December 24, 2003

Wow, three years have come and gone already! So many things are different now than they were back then. My mom and I get along much better even though we have our days. I also now know what true love feels like, and I still can't believe my brother is engaged!

My parents and I went to Mass without Philip this year. It seems like anymore he's too embarrassed to be seen with the family in public. That's OK; I have shit on him that I can tell his friends if he pisses me off enough!

Gampa and Gamma are coming tomorrow as always. I can't wait. It's been a while since we've seen them. It sucks they have to live so far.

I just finished up meditating a few minutes ago. I prayed that Mike wouldn't get too lonely and have a great Christmas. I also prayed for his family. That he might be able to find them again someday.

Well as I say every year Merry Christmas to all and to all a good night!

January 3, 2004

Break has gone by way too quick. We only have three days until we go back. I guess it's not so bad. I will get to see Mike more and hang out with my friends before school and at lunch.

Some more good news, I might be getting a job! Wendy's is hiring, so all I have to do is fill out an application and wait. It will be nice if I get it because I need the money to put back in my savings and have a little to have fun with as well.

January 10, 2004

Break has been over now for four days, but it's the weekend again, so I have a couple more days of freedom.

Here's what's new. A week ago, I learned that two kids from school were killed in a car crash on New Year's Day. According to the news, they were on their way back from a church lock-in and the boy who was driving fell asleep at the wheel and they hit a tree. The boy was pronounced dead at the scene, and his sister who I knew from art class, died shortly after arriving at the hospital.

The day school started back up, the mood was very somber. People were crying, and the guidance office was full all day. We even had a moment of silence during the morning announcements, to remember them. My mom and I were going to go to the funeral, but my mom bailed at the last minute because it was snowing.

In other news, Mike has court again on Wednesday, and we are hoping he gets emancipated soon. Thank God, he has his old case worker back. She doesn't have her head stuck up her ass and lets him do more. She also knows how to fight for things and not fart around about it.

As I always say, prayer changes things. He is really making good progress and never gets in trouble. What really sucks about the treatment center though is that sometimes when his roommates do something wrong, they all get LOP (Loss of Privileges). He has been doing excellent either than that. He's even doing good in school, and he hasn't had any tardies or referrals in a long time.

January 17, 2004

Will the deaths ever stop? Why can't it be births? Now my family and I are on our way back from Grandma Becca's funeral. She died Wednesday, which was January 14. We will all miss her but I guess it was her time to go. She lived a full life, considering she was ninety-six.

This has been the saddest month on record for me, starting with the two kids that died in the tragic crash on New Year's. Then came Philip's friend Chris's two brothers that were killed in a house fire. That was really sad because they were so young and they touched so many people. Then last Tuesday, a good friend from church passed away, and then Wednesday, we got the news about Grandma.

Onto the better things, Mike learned at court that he should be getting emancipated in July as long as he stays out of trouble. So far so good! He is still behaving. His case worker also pushed to have me added to his phone list so we can keep contact outside of school. His judge also suggested that he go for his GED, but his teacher of record says no. He wants Mike to stay in the classes he's in now because he's afraid the other will be too hard.

January 25, 2004

Life is getting busier once again, so here's the scoop. Mike, as far as I know, is fine. He unfortunately doesn't call me every day, and it's Saturday, so I haven't talked to him since school on Friday.

Right now, it's snowing out, and we are supposed to get five to seven inches. I hope we get a two-hour delay tomorrow considering we haven't had one this year and this is the biggest snowstorm we have had yet this season.

February 1, 2004

We finally got a snow day last Tuesday, and Monday, we had a two-hour delay like I was hoping! Unfortunately,

Tuesday was the day we had a case conference scheduled. We rescheduled it for this coming up Friday instead.

The reason for the conference you ask? I am having some problems in a couple of my classes, so I'm going to see if my teacher of record, Mr. Jay, can switch my schedule around and, hopefully, get me into some better classes so I can get more help. I have him for pre-algebra, and I am really struggling in there. Sometimes, he can be a little bit of an ass, but he's not as bad as the witch I had last year!

I'm currently watching the Super Bowl and the Patriots are ahead, boooooooo! I hate Tom Brady!

February 6, 2004

I'm babysitting again, except this time Katrina is here to help me out. She makes it more fun because she knows the kids better as they are her cousins after all. I have, however, grown a lot closer to them considering I have been watching them since October.

We had another two-hour delay today. Thank God, we thought ahead and scheduled my conference for the afternoon because we would have had to reschedule again! My teacher was actually decent to work with today. He switched a couple of my classes around so I can be with Mike more. I'm just glad this guy is willing to work with me when I need help!

Tomorrow, I am going to my friend Emmy's birthday party at the bowling alley. After that, my daddy is taking Katrina and I to the "Jam the John" women's basketball game at Ball State! Admission is only $1, and they are trying to see how many people they can jam into the John Worthen Arena!

Then Sunday, my daddy and I are going rock climbing with the youth group in Indy! This is going to be fun because I've never been before.

February 24, 2004

Rock climbing was a blast! I did fall once because my partner had too much slack in the rope, but I just picked myself up and went on.

Last Friday, I stayed the night for the first time with my friend Amber. We ate pizza and watched some movies. When it came time to go to bed, I had a little bit of trouble falling asleep because she lives right next to the train tracks, but once I got to sleep, I slept all night.

This coming up weekend, she is going with me to fast with the youth group. This will be my second year. Thank God, this time we are all staying together the whole time. If you will remember last year we had to go home on Friday night and go back on Saturday morning. That was torture because my mom ate right in front of me. This will make time go a hell of a lot faster and it will sure as hell not be as hard.

March 3, 2004

I'm now in the psych hospital once again. I decided to admit myself because I was thinking about slitting my wrists and ending it all. The stress of everything has piled up to the point of no way out.

Katrina told Mike yesterday about my thoughts, and he started throwing a bitch fit! We had a really big discussion that ended up in the guidance counselor's office, where she explained to him, so he could understand. He finally calmed down, and then the counselor dismissed me to go home for the rest of the day. Then today, my parents got me in here for a psych evaluation, and that's when the doctor decided that I needed to be admitted.

I really miss Mike right now, but I know that the harder I work here, the faster I get out to see him. I will keep you posted.

March 8, 2004

I'm still here in the hospital, but I'm starting to feel better every day. The food here is OK, but it's definitely not like home. I did have a roommate, but she left today. Now when I go into the room, it's too damn quiet. The first night I was here, staff had to keep telling us to shut up and go to sleep, but we couldn't because we had so much in common. She also has a boyfriend, who is very close, just like me, and he proposed to her right before she came here!

Speaking of boyfriends, Mike has been calling my parents every day to see how I'm doing. I'm also starting to miss my other friends at school.

That brings me to my next subject; school here is only two hours a day! If only school was that way all the time! That would be great!

I'm hoping to get out of here before my daddy's birthday. It's in three days, and this is the year he turns the big fifty! I want to be there. Unfortunately, because of money, I couldn't throw the big party I wanted to. It sucks because he deserves it!

March 21, 2004

I've been out of the hospital for about a week now, and I feel like a million bucks!

It's the beginning of spring break already! I'm at Grandma Karla's, celebrating the March birthdays with my family. That reminds me that I unfortunately didn't get out in time to celebrate with Daddy. That's OK though; I didn't miss much because he had to work that day anyway. I did, however get to talk to him on the phone, which was cool.

Tomorrow, my parents and I are going up to Chicago to see Daddy's friend Matt, from college. We are also going to have a little fun while we are there. I am so excited because this is the first time we have ever been on vacation for spring break! It will be nice to get away from the hellhole we call Muncie, Indiana, and on our way back, since Lafayette is on the way, my parents are dropping me off at Gampa and Gamma's, so I can spend three days there. Then Gampa and Gamma are taking me home Saturday afternoon.

Chapter Fourteen

Spring 2004

March 26, 2004

I was so busy in Chicago that I didn't have a chance to write. Here's what we did.

Monday, as we were driving up there, we stopped at the mall in Hobart, Indiana. We walked around for a little bit, and my mom and I did a little shopping in the process. I was in need of a new pair of shoes, so we went into one of my favorite stores and found some that I loved. After I picked them out, I looked around that store for a little longer and ended up buying a pack of barbwire jelly bracelets that came with a matching necklace and earrings that all glow in the dark. By that time, we were ready to hit the road again.

We hit Chicago just in time for rush hour. That was interesting, but with Daddy behind the wheel, we got to our destination in one piece. Our arrival time was around 7:00 p.m. Chicago time

(8:00 p.m. in Indiana). His wife already had dinner waiting for us, and you talk about a rich meal. She is Lithuanian, and in her house, if you don't get enough to eat, then it's your own damn fault because there's always plenty!

Matt had to work until 10:00 p.m., so we visited for a while with his wife and got to know her a little better since Mom has never met her and Daddy and I haven't seen them since the wedding in 1999. When he finally got home, he walked in, said hi, hit the shower, then we sat down and caught up on old times until 1:00 a.m!

Tuesday, Matt had taken the day off work so he could go with us and enjoy Chicago. It was an advantage because, instead of trying to find a place to park, we were allowed to at his sister's costume shop. From there, she took us to the Sears Tower. We went up to the top and stayed for a good two hours. After that, we were starving, so we walked a few blocks and found a real Chicago style pizza parlor. We had a stuffed pizza that was so filling I only ate one piece! When we got done there, we walked around a little more to see what else there was, and we stumbled upon the ESPN Zone. We went in there and I challenged everybody to air hockey. I beat all three of them! I wanted to play more, but Mom said no. When we went to the restroom, right before we left I looked up, and there were TVs over every stall! That cracked me up. I guess that gives you something to do when you're stuck there for a while.

It was starting to get dark when we came out of there, so we headed back to the L train, waited for it, and by the time we got back to the van, we could see the Chicago skyline. We then started heading back to Matt's house, and as I was singing along to my CD player, he was teasing me. He asked what I did with the money my daddy gave me for singing lessons. I turned it off after that, and we talked and joked around some more.

On Wednesday, Matt had to go back to work, so we were on our own. We spent pretty much all day at the Museum of Science and Industry. That was one of the best museums my daddy has ever taken us to. I learned things, but in a fun way. The last one we went to before this was in Washington DC, and it was too boring. We even went to the IMAX Theater, and that was really kick ass. I wish we had one of those closer to home that we could watch regular movies on. That would be awesome!

Thursday morning, we left, and here I sit now. It's Friday. Today, Gampa and Gamma took me to a ceramic place. I picked out a bear that I named MC for Muncie Central. I painted her the school colors—purple and white—and I put a paw print on her belly to represent the bearcat. Now all that's left to do is put her in the kiln and make her glaze. The lady that's in charge there said she will be ready in a week, so, unfortunately, I can't see my finished product until the next time we meet up with Gampa and Gamma.

I wish I could stay here until Sunday, but my parents won't let me. I guess they want me to get settled before school starts. I hate it when they do this to me. Like I've said before, I love it so much up here. I wish my parents would move us up here. There are more jobs here, the crime rate is lower, the schools are a hell of a lot better and there is all together more to do around here and it doesn't cost as much if at all!

April 3, 2004

Boy, does my life keep getting better or what? Now I'm at the Black Bear Inn in Berne, Indiana, with Amber and her mom. We have been here since yesterday. We left town right after school. Here, in a little while, we are going to the mall in Fort Wayne, to have some fun.

More good news, Mike had a case conference in Lafayette with his caseworker over break and he happened to run into his aunt and uncle. They told him that his youngest brother has been adopted. He and his caseworker talked about it, and she is supposed to be arranging a visit sometime soon.

My parents are doing great. Life at home is very peaceful at the moment. Philip, as usual, is the same old butt munch. He keeps to himself and stays in his room on the computer except when he's at work.

April 7, 2004

Oh my god! You will never guess what happened today! Mike finally popped the question! You know the answer was yes, and where he did it was perfect. He walked me to the bottom of the stairs on the east side of the student center and made sure all my friends were around to watch! Now it's official! He has asked me to marry him, and he has given me a ring. That ring symbolizes trust, honesty, loyalty, and, above all, love!

I can't believe that a little over a year ago I didn't know if I would ever find somebody! Now look at me! What a difference a year can make!

This relationship has changed me in a lot of ways. It has made me grow up pretty fast, and I now want my independence! I don't need him every five seconds. It has also changed him. He is now staying out of trouble for the most part and making me worry a lot less.

Now, to get through the rest of high school and graduate on time, so we can get married! I can't wait to start my life with him!

April 18, 2004

Mike has court again on Wednesday, but first, on Tuesday, he's going on a field trip with one of his classes, to Fort Wayne. They are going to the mall, and I am so jealous. I can't complain though; they do deserve it after all. This is his job placement class we're talking about. He said he would bring me something home, so that helps. It still sucks that I will be stuck in class all day, while he's having fun!

Tomorrow, we have another half day, and as usual, Katrina is coming home with me on the bus. I'm not sure what we're going to do yet. It's supposed to be nice, so we might go for a bike ride on the bike trail.

April 25, 2004

I'm on my way back from another youth retreat, this time in Kokomo. My mom was the chaperone for this one, and Amber and I were the only people to go from our youth group. We paired up with the Benton County group from Sacred Heart Fowler and St. Patrick's Oxford. They were a group of eight including the chaperone, all girls. I also thought it was cool that I was hanging out with some of my daddy's classmates' daughters because Benton County is where he's from, Fowler to be exact.

In not so good news, Mike ended up not getting to go to Ft. Wayne because one of the stupid girls at the treatment center purposely wrote a false report that he had supposedly threatened to rape her all because she was jealous and she didn't want him to go on that field trip. When his bus got there and he didn't get off, I knew something was wrong, and sure enough, a girl came running over and said, "Mike's not coming to school today. He's on supervised LOP!" As soon as I heard that, I was furious! He had worked so hard to not be able to go, and for that Bitch to ruin it for him was just sick!

That made it so I didn't get to see him until Thursday. I was so relieved to see his face. I ran up to him so fast I almost knocked him down. We then walked hand in hand into the cafeteria, got into line to get breakfast, and sat down to catch up! He told me that Tuesday sucked. He just sat there and thought about me all day. Then Wednesday, the incident was brought up in court. Both the judge and his case worker looked at staff like they were nuts! They've known Mike long enough to know that he would admit it if he did something like that.

The good news; Mike gets to move back into the group home on May 20 and stay until August 4. After that, he will be emancipated. I have, however, reminded him several times that he better not screw up at all because, after August, if he does, he will go to the big house (jail). I trust him though, considering he has now been out of serious trouble for five months.

May 12, 2004

Mike and I get to go to the prom this year! It's coming up on Saturday. I'm getting my nails and hair done professionally so I can look pretty for him. The best thing about this is Mike was able to move back to the group home early because his behavior has been excellent!

I have been so busy lately that I haven't had a chance to write. Life has been so stressful lately that I picked up smoking again. My parents don't know because I do it either when I'm at a friend's house or when Katrina and I are taking a walk.

May 16, 2004

Prom was awesome. We had the night of our lives. Unfortunately, we weren't able to go to after prom because he hasn't been at the group home for two weeks yet.

The school year is almost over again. Only eleven more days left until summer break. I have a good feeling this one is going to be a lot better than last! Mike's attitude has definitely come a long way in the past six months. That's exactly what we want. He's very positive now.

I'm babysitting again, but they are asleep. We went to the park today, and I guess I wore their butts out.

May 23, 2004

I'm sitting here at Katrina's on the porch, watching her and Martha swim. The reason I'm not in there is because it's only 10:00 a.m. and it's still kind of chilly. I'm waiting until this afternoon.

Joe's open house was yesterday, and a lot of her teachers were there. I guess you can say she's a teachers' pet. However I really have no room to talk because I was that way with Mrs. Fraley.

In other news, I don't think I have to babysit tonight because Katrina's aunt is working the day shift today. That will just give me more time with Katrina. I think she wants me to stay another night anyway.

Last but not least, I now have a country idol! Gretchen Wilson! She just came out with a song called "Redneck Woman," and it describes me to a T. Gretchen is definitely a redneck woman herself, doing some four wheeling and going "Muddin" with her truck! I can't wait to see her in concert!

May 31, 2004

Breaking News! Philip and Joe broke it off! No I didn't stutter! It really happened! I couldn't believe it!

It started like this. They came out of Philip's room with tears in their eyes. I thought to myself, "This is odd?" Then I got a call from Katrina, and she told me all about it. There's way too much to go into detail, so all I will say is it wasn't meant to be. You won't believe this one, but Philip actually talked to my mom for a little bit, but she had to ask him questions first.

Onto better things, I convinced my parents to let me get my ears double pierced yesterday. They finally gave in after I had been begging them several months.

The Indy 500 was also yesterday, but it got cut a tad short due to tornado warnings for all of Marion County. There were seventeen reports of tornados in Indiana alone.

Mike is still doing really great! I have a lot of confidence that he's going to get out on time for once! We are growing closer every day. It may not make much sense, but when we have our arguments, it makes us stronger because we just make up and things are even better than before! I guess it's not once you think about it!

June 9, 2004

More bad news! Another one of my classmates has died. This guy and I go way back to the first grade. In fact, he was my first crush ever! He was struck by a car on his moped and died at the scene, and he was only sixteen! Now his twin brother lives in his honor.

Onto the good things, I am now in driver's education. Mom is supposed to take me to get my permit tomorrow because I have to have it to practice with my class.

Half the school is being forced to take summer classes this year because the stupid computer system had a glitch and messed up people's schedules! Mike happens to be one of those people, and the thing that gets me is they have no special education classes, so how do they expect our people to be able to pass? I don't know?

Enough on that subject and onto other things; Mike still hasn't got to have any home visits yet, even though he's been on his best behavior. They have different staff this time, and one of them, in particular, is an ass to everybody. He won't let anybody do anything, and it pisses me off!

June 20, 2004

Today is Father's Day, so we went to the movies, and then went swimming in the pool to cool off because it's hotter than hell out!

On Friday, I went to see Tracey Lawrence in concert in Lafayette with my aunt Clarice. I stood by up by the stage the whole time and was lucky enough to catch a ribbon that he dropped purposely off a bouquet of flowers. I now have it tied around my purse strap for good luck.

I haven't talked to Mike all weekend, and for some strange reason, he called Grandma Karla's house, thinking I was there. I guess he got things confused when I said I was going out of town, and he must have thought I meant Martinsville. I am, however, still a bit worried because he hasn't called back at all, but deep down inside, I know everything will be fine. I just worry damn too much!

I do have my permit now and the picture; well, I have taken much better. That's not the point of it though. That brings me to my other fun adventure that I had Friday, before we left for Lafayette. My driving instructor took me along with two of my other classmates on our first practice drive. We went to the fairgrounds, and when it came my turn, I was a nervous wreck the whole time. It's kind of like the first time I learned to ride my bike, without the training wheels. You've got to learn how to keep your wheels straight. I can do this, but it's going to take a while because of my depth perception. It sucks!

Chapter Fifteen

Summer 2004

June 30, 2004

Mom is making me more nervous with this driving thing! I would rather have Daddy teach me than her. Every time she is in the car with me, she screams literally every time I make a mistake. She doesn't seem to understand the concept of screaming makes it worse and can cause wrecks. My daddy on the other hand is a lot calmer and helps by explaining things in a way that helps me learn what I need to know to be able to pass the road test. It's coming up this Friday, and I'm not sure if I am ready. I'm definitely a lot slower than everybody else, as usual.

In other news, Mike tore something in his ankle, playing basketball last week, so now we are taking him to and from classes. He still hasn't been able to add me to his visit list, but we are just thankful for what we do have. At least there's the phone.

July 3, 2004

Mom is still on my nerves, but not as bad. I guess Daddy had another talk with her. My daddy has also been the one teaching me how to drive. The bad news is I didn't pass the road test, so now I have to wait for a while to take it at the license branch. I'm really in no hurry. I am going to make sure I have a lot of practice because I don't want to have my license for just a short time and then get into a serious wreck.

Right now, I'm in the car with Grandma Sue and Grandpa Earnie (Amber's grandparents). We're on our way to a birthday party in Geneva, Indiana.

Where's Amber you ask? She's with her boyfriend and Mom. They are going to a Kiss and Poison concert tonight in Noblesville. I was going, but Mike called me last night and told me I had finally been added to his visit list and I was allowed to come see him tonight. We have been waiting so long for this, so I ended up giving my ticket to Amber's boyfriend.

Wow, I just looked up, and we are really out in the sticks. There's nothing but road and cornfields ahead!

July 13, 2004

This is really rare, but now I miss my mom! I haven't seen her for almost a week now because I've been with Amber and her family.

The first place we went was Nashville, Indiana, last weekend. They have a wide variety of outdoor shops, but because they aren't handicap accessible, we didn't shop too long because Grandma Sue's scooter wouldn't fit into any of the stores which made me angry. They need to move up into the twenty-first century and modernize things so people who are in wheel chairs can enjoy the fun shit too.

The rest of the weekend was basically spent in the pool which was pretty neat. It was in what looked like a garage with the doors and everything. It also went to eight feet so we could dive and do cannon balls. We also spent a whole bunch of time in the game room. They had a claw machine that was easy to win beanie babies out of.

Then Sunday went back through Muncie, dropped Grandpa Earnie off, picked Amber's boyfriend up, while I visited with Mike for a couple of hours, and finally drove up here to Goshen where we have been commuting back and forth to Shipshewana, Indiana, the last two days to get to the giant outdoor flea market. I've bought some interesting stuff including a dream catcher something I've been trying to get my hands on for years. We've also been swimming at the hotel. This pool goes to ten feet, and it's bigger than the one in Nashville. We were fixing to go swimming a few minutes ago, but as soon as got out there, the hotel staff rushed us out because there was really bad lightning, even though it's an indoor pool.

I'm definitely missing Mike for sure at this point. I know he's doing great though because he and my mom have been talking on the phone every day, so that makes it so I can relax. I think he might have tried to call me earlier tonight, but because of the storms in the area, the cell phones aren't getting good reception. It's all good. I'm probably going to see him tomorrow anyway because we are leaving to go home in the morning.

Mike's case worker has been saying that he might possibly be moving into his own apartment on his birthday, which is July 29 if you didn't remember. That means only sixteen more days until he's considered an adult and no longer a juvenile!

July 16, 2004

Mike is hanging in there as every day passes. I do believe that he is finally at the end of his extremely hard, rough road and can see the light out of that long dark tunnel. In less than two weeks, he will be free! I just pray that he doesn't go insane between now and then from his roommates trying to give him a hard time.

Tomorrow when he comes over for his home visit, he wants me to cut his hair with the new pair of clippers I just bought. My thought is **Yay, my first hair-cutting job! Hope I don't screw it up!**

My mom just came in my room, and she's showing me the smiley-face umbrella she just bought me. It's really cute.

July 26, 2004

Another Bearcat has fallen. This time it was the former basketball coach of twenty-five years or something like that who was recently forced to resign for stupid reasons. Everybody was shocked when they heard the news because it was so sudden. His calling hours were today, and a bunch of the teachers and faculty were there.

Now onto better things; Mike is doing great. Unfortunately, he doesn't get to move on his birthday after all. To top that off, they are moving him to Connersville, which is over an hour away. There are positives though. He will get so much more freedom with phone calls, and visits will actually get to be overnight now. We have already made it certain that he will be going to Holiday World with us for the Shipman activity day in a couple of weeks. After that, we are going home with Gampa and Gamma and staying in Lafayette for a few days.

July 31, 2004

I'm on my way back from Grandma Karla's. We are celebrating Mike's birthday today because he has been approved for a six-hour home visit. We are having a cookout with burgers and all that good junk, and Mom has also made him a cake. We are also going to swim, probably from right after he gets there until dinner because it's hot, and this will be the first time he has been able to swim in my pool.

Something I have to tell you before I forget; while I was down at Grandma's this time, we made a trip down to Nashville, Indiana. I got a chance to check out some of the shops that I didn't have a chance to a couple of weeks ago.

August 10, 2004

We're now on our way back from Holiday World! We had a great time. It was, however, hot, and the lines were longer than usual, and to stay cool, we hit the water park after lunch and stayed there pretty much all afternoon. They have some of the best water slides ever, and the wave pool is really kick ass. It's also not a day at Holiday World until I get my Dippin' Dot fix. We've been going there since I was three or four years old, and I've got to have them every time!

Oh, by the way, I'm not driving for a really long time after today. About an hour ago, my daddy let me drive, and we're in the van, right? Well, we were on a very curvy road, and as I was rounding one curve, I didn't turn my wheel sharp enough and I nearly missed a pick-up truck head-on! I'm still trying to relax from that one, and I'm really sore from what really seemed to me like a white knuckle drive!

Mike still hasn't moved yet because the bastards from Medicaid haven't finished up his paperwork yet. His judge said that she will make it priority to get him out by September 1. She's sick of people farting around too. It pisses me off so bad, but at least he was allowed to go on this trip. It sucks that he has to be back by 10:00 p.m.! Curfews are so overrated!

August 23, 2004

It's been a busy thirteen days since I last wrote. I'm preparing for my junior year and enjoying these last three days of summer break.

Right now, it's 1:00 a.m.! I'm going to miss staying up late and sleeping in. I will definitely have some great summer stories to tell my school friends on Thursday. I have already gotten my schedule, and they have me in Mr. Jay's class three times a day. Mom says hell no and so do I. He stresses me out too much.

Mike is doing great and still getting sweeter by the day.

September 3, 2004

We are on our way to Connersville to get Mike! Grrrrr, this road is getting a little bumpy, so hang on!

Now it's better! I hate construction on the back roads. The stupid thing even messed my new CD up!

We just crossed from Randolph into Wayne County. That means we are almost there; one more to go. I can't wait to get there so he can show me his house. He also has two roommates I would like to meet.

I finally got my schedule changed, and I am no longer on diploma track because the schoolwork is stressing me out too bad. They now have me in the job placement class that Mike was in last year. I'm really hoping to find a job soon, so that way I can stay busy.

Next weekend, there's another youth retreat. This one is the annual J-Fest in Noblesville. Mike is coming to that as well. My daddy is a chaperone again, along with three of the other adults in charge of our youth group.

September 11, 2004

It's been three years already since the world came to a complete halt as we all watched America take a beating that would go down in history, to be on a scale much larger than Pearl Harbor. Many still have yet to find peace due to the fact that Bin Laden is still at large. I myself pray daily that they find him soon, so justice will be served for everybody!

Speaking of prayer I'm currently at J-Fest, winding down from a long day of worship and praise! During Eucharistic Adoration earlier this evening, I laid out all my stuff to the Lord, as usual. I prayed for all the men and women fighting for our country and their families, asked for him to bless Mike and me with our relationship, and also prayed like hell for forgiveness and other good stuff. It didn't seem like it, but I meditated for an hour and a half. Let me tell you, the Lord is powerful, and if you believe, he can and will take your stresses away!

Before this weekend, I hadn't been feeling myself. My mom and I have been fighting a lot again. After this weekend, however, I feel like there's a lot to look forward to. I'm hoping I can take the stuff I learned home with me and use it in everyday life!

Tomorrow, we have to get up again at 7:00 a.m. like we did today. We will have breakfast, and then they will probably have us jam out some more to wake us up. After a little bit of that, they will probably have another speaker or two. Then at 11:00 a.m. is Mass. Finally, we all get into our car groups, go somewhere to eat, and head home.

September 15, 2004

I'm having some serious social problems. Amber is being a real pain in the butt. She started stealing Rhianna's lunch the other day when she had gotten up to go to the throw something away. Then, when the teacher confronted her she denied it. It pissed of me and Rhianna both!

Then yesterday afternoon, Grandma Sue called me and said not to be hanging around Amber anymore because I have too much of an attitude. That really makes no sense at all. I wasn't trying to start drama. I was just trying to help my other friend out, and I definitely don't have an attitude. Besides, Amber's the one who's always getting in trouble at school. Whatever it's not worth shitting a brick over.

Onto better things, homecoming is this week. Tomorrow is White Tee Day, but the problem is I still have no plain white tees. For spirit day Friday, I'm going to dye my hair purple and paint my face for the game. Daddy is picking Mike up so he can be here in time for the game.

Chapter Sixteen

Fall 2004

September 22, 2004

Welcome back to my living hell! I'm even more stressed now than I was before. They're still making me take the stupid I-Step test even though I don't understand a damn thing that's going on! Another thing that gets me down is that Mike can't come up this weekend. My mom and I got into about the way my hair was done for picture day, and I told her off. To top it all off, I just found out from my principal that Mike is not allowed to go to Sadie's because he doesn't go to our school. Well, I have news for that bastard! Philip went last year and they said nothing! It also pissed me off when the assistant principal had the balls to tell Mike he had to leave the homecoming dance halfway through, all because he wasn't a student. Ever since that new assistant principal has come to this school, nobody is allowed to have fun anymore! It's a bunch of bullshit! We can't even have a conversation in the halls during passing period without him ease dropping. Hell, the other day, when Katrina and I got into a little disagreement, I told her to bite my ass, and I didn't even realize he was standing there until I heard, "My office now!" Then I looked at him and quickly ran away to his office in tears, pissed at myself for what just happened. I ended up getting after-school detention.

I guess you can say in general I have had one hell of a shitty week. I'm just hoping the rest of the damn thing goes better.

September 30, 2004

Dang, it's almost October already? This means Mike has been out of trouble for almost a year now. It will be exactly a month from tomorrow. That also marks the day Fred has been with me for four years.

Life is getting much better now. My depression streak is finally over and I'm back to my normal self again.

Friday we have a conference with Mike, his case manager and his house staff. Then he's coming home for another exciting fun-filled weekend here in the great town we call Muncie, Indiana!

October 2, 2004

My life sucks. Mike has his eyes glued to the game he is playing and not paying any attention to me! I feel invisible.

A few minutes ago, I was trying to clean the family room, and he comes barging in demanding everything his way! I had put the TV where I wouldn't trip over it, so I could put the card table up for our romantic dinner, but now he's hogging up all the space and he put the TV back so I can't do anything! I am pissed! He is being a selfish little bastard and he knows it! What comes first, damn it, the game or me?

October 4, 2004

I'm sitting here on my bed trying to wind down from my day. It's 9:56 p.m. I was supposed to be in bed at nine thirty, but I was taking a shower. I'm also running behind due to the fact that I had a lot of homework tonight.

Mike stopped playing his game shortly after I finished writing on Saturday. He realized how pissed I really was and couldn't stand it anymore. We finally settled down and ate our dinner of spaghetti and salad, then watched a movie.

Sunday is my least favorite day now. That's the day we have to make the trip back to Connersville and drop Mike off. The ride home seems so long. Then it's five more days of long distance phone calls because my parents are too cheap to invest in unlimited long distance calls or cell phones.

October 6, 2004

I can't take these emotions anymore! I feel like cutting again! Every time I think the depression and anger is gone for good, it comes back with a vengeance! I am going completely insane! This is never going to end! Stuff just keeps on happening all at once, and I can't handle it! I don't know what to do anymore, and it seems like neither does anybody else! I need help now, not tomorrow, not Friday, immediately, ASAP!

What people don't seem to understand is the fact of how bad I really feel! They just prescribe me another medicine and expect me to give it four to six weeks to take its full effect. Bull freaking shit! These feelings have gone on way too long, and I need to feel at least somewhat better in the next week, not the next month! I'm so sick of having to wait, but there's really nothing else I can do right now. This is Muncie, Indiana! We have the saddest excuse of doctors ever known to mankind!

October 12, 2004

I'm doing much better since the last time I wrote. I talked out things with my counselor and she helped to calm my nerves a bit.

In other news, Mike has to start coming every other weekend now. The gas is getting too expensive for my parents. That and my mom got herself a job, working at a group home on the weekends. She's working the graveyard of all things, and my parents are sharing one car because my brother is using the other one for work!

Before I forget, I ran into Joe today, and it turns out her and my brother's friend Chris are an item now. I know what you're thinking, awkward! Now they are moving to Ohio together because I guess he got a job.

October 20, 2004

My life is so messed up again. The doctors are freaking with my meds.

Oh yeah, freak is my word of the day. I've used it a million times since I woke up. God only knows what freaking word I'm going to wake up with in my head tomorrow! It usually depends on my dreams.

Last night I had a dream that terrorists flew a plane into the hospital here in Muncie and it killed a bunch of people. Then they took the neighborhoods hostage with shotguns, and one of them got into my house through an unlocked window. He ended up finding me under the table and shot me in my leg. The last word I remember saying before I woke up was "freak."

In other freaking news, Mike only gets to stay one freaking night this weekend because of the whole Mom and Dad job-car situation. This freaking sucks! I can't wait until Christmas so we can spend some quality time together without rushing things. The weekends go way too freaking fast! Freaking A!

November 2, 2004

One more week until I'm seventeen! Wow, that means one more until I'm an adult! I can't wait! I'll be able to get tattoos and body piercings without my parents' permission, vote, and pretty much do whatever I diddly damn well please as long as I follow the laws!

Life keeps on getting harder and harder by the day. I miss Mike like hell. I really wish his case manager would hurry up and get him into a waiver home up here. I need him so bad right now because it seems like he's the only one who understands me anymore.

I'm feeling invisible to the rest of the world again. It feels like my parents don't care enough about me when they don't push for my rights. When I come to them with a problem, especially school related, they either give me advice that never works or just talk to my teachers who know almost nothing about me outside of school and like to assume things. My parents need to stand up for me a lot more. There's not a lot I can do; I'm still considered a kid.

I have a lot of emotional issues getting in the way of my schoolwork, and nobody seems to be listening. They all just think I'm trying to get attention. Well, guess what? For their info, I am not! It's getting so bad I have a hell of a time just getting out of bed in the morning. God help me! I don't know what else to do!

November 4, 2004

Life is still hell! Yesterday, my doctor saw me and agreed that I was in no condition to go to school, so she wrote an excuse for me to have the rest of the week off. Now I'm just relaxing, doing what I feel like. The good thing is tomorrow is Friday, and Daddy doesn't have to work, so we get to pick Mike up a day early! That really makes me a happy camper. He also gets to stay until Wednesday because of my birthday being on Tuesday!

More bad news, Katrina and I are now enemies again. She claims Mike wants to have sex with her when in reality we all know its vice-versa. She just likes to start drama.

November 14, 2004

Seventeen is the shit! I am finally legally able to watch R-rated movies. In fact, my mom, Mike, and I all watched one on my birthday!

Katrina and I are still not cool. Her and Martha thought it would be funny to go into the locker room when Ashlee and

I were swimming during the pep session last week and hide my purse in a locker all because I didn't want to listen to what Katrina had to say about Mike.

I freaked when I couldn't find it at first. Then I became suspicious, and I was pretty sure who was behind it. When my mom picked me up from school that day, Mike was in the van with her and I told them about it. We immediately went to Katrina's house and talked to her mom, who had no knowledge of what happened but said she would talk to her daughter.

A week went by. And still nothing until Friday. Mom picked me up, we went home, and I did my routine. Then about three forty-five, the doorbell rang. It was Katrina and her parents. She had come to confess and now I have to wait until Monday to get the thing because the school was already locked Friday, and if my purse was not there, somebody is really going to pay!

Now to more pleasant things, I just started kickboxing classes, my first one being Friday night. My instructor Richard has a dummy that we can practice on called Bob. I acted like he was Katrina. My legs are still sore and that was two nights ago.

I'm also taking care of my baby for child development class this weekend. Her name is Kaylee Rebecca. She's like a real baby except when she cries all I have to do is stick a key into her back and hold it there until she coos. The first time she cried I wasn't sure how to work the key, and I couldn't get her to quit crying. That was when I was on my way into kickboxing. Richard just laughed and said, "That's what real babies do!" Later that night, Mike and I went over to a friend's house to stay the night, and she showed me how it was done. I'm actually going to miss her when I have to take her back in the morning. I am kind of wondering, though, how I did as a mommy?

November 23, 2004

It seems like an eternity since I last wrote. I was admitted to another psych hospital on the sixteenth, and they wouldn't let me write. You would think that being in the hospital they would encourage it, but they're ass holes there. Hell, they took my clothes away and made me wear scrubs like I was in prison or something. They make the last place I was at look like the Hilton!

I know one thing if I ever have be admitted again I will not be going back there! Their food was nasty, and I got almost no exercise, and what pissed me off the most was if I was having trouble sleeping, I would go up to the nurse's station and they would tell me to shut up and go back to bed. I'm just thanking God I'm out of there!

November 27, 2004

These stupid meds they put me on when I was in the hospital are giving me worse mood swings and are making me fat. I'm crying over the stupidest things and I always have an uneasy feeling I can never get rid of. As you can see, it is giving me tremors as well, so bad that I can barely write.

Onto the positives, we put up our Christmas tree today, although it really doesn't feel like the holidays yet. My biggest fear is that everybody is going to be fighting this year because my parents have a lot of bills. Our insurance hasn't been paying anything when it comes to mental health.

Oh great, here we go again! I'm having another mood swing episode, from happy to shitty in 2 seconds! I hate these feelings of irritation. This is the worst I've ever felt. I've got to get this fixed soon. I'm scared if I don't that I will be like this forever and that definitely can't happen! I want to be me again!

December 2, 2004

I'm feeling a little better now. They got me off the Remeron, which was making me gain all the weight, but I'm still on Geodon. I'm still feeling uneasy, and now I'm having serious issues sleeping. I also still have really bad tremors and am hyper all the time. I know I didn't get enough exercise today, but yesterday, I ran around for four hours and still wasn't a bit tired, then went to kick boxing and still nothing!

In other news, Martha is officially the biggest bitch in the world! She stole Rhianna's wallet today and, of course, denied it like most thieves do. We searched everywhere and could never find it either. We think she must have taken it with her and disposed of it off school grounds.

She and Katrina are a match made in hell. They are all buddy-buddy now, so we are still not talking, not even a hello when we pass each other in the hallway. I hate it because she sits by me in Child Development. I try not to even look at her, but she likes to bitch that I'm hogging up all the table space with my books and purse. That just makes me want to smack the shit out of her cocky ass!

She thinks she's so tough and she can push me around like I'm her dog or something, and until she quits hanging out with Martha and figures out for herself what a no good, lying, cheating, stealing, psycho moocher she is, I will have nothing to do with her!

December 5, 2004

I am scared to death. I can't find my ring. I took it off last night at kickboxing and haven't seen it since. Mike says we can get another one; it's no big deal because it wasn't real, but that's not the point. If I lost this one, I'm scared I will lose the real diamond.

I'm sure as you can tell the doctor still hasn't changed my meds yet. My primary physician can't get ahold of the jackass who prescribed them to me in the hospital and the fact that last

Friday night I was at Amber's house when we had to call my daddy at two in the morning because I was having a seizure.

What I don't understand is why my regular doctor can't change things without talking to the people at the hospital first. They are farting around way too long. It's getting to the point where I feel like I could collapse any second and I could die. I feel so weak to where I can't stand five seconds without holding on to something. I've got to feel better soon! I've just got to!

December 18, 2004

My meds are finally regulated again. Well, about the same as before I went into the hospital. The hospital didn't help at all. All they did was made me a zombie and send me on my way. I think they need to be shut down because they don't give anybody the care they need. They basically do to everybody what they just did to me. Everybody is given the similar diagnoses, drugged up, and sent home.

Enough on those assholes, I'm just glad to be feeling at least down to earth again! My regular doctor was never able to get ahold of the stupid hospital people, so she finally decided to use her best judgment and move on with things.

I no longer feel like I'm going to collapse, I'm finally getting my sleep again, I'm not as hyper all the time, and as you can tell, my tremors are completely gone. Emotionally, I'm not doing so hot yet. Mike thinks I keep getting an attitude when in reality he's the one being an ass.

I can't believe it's almost Christmas. We are going to Aunt Teresa's house tomorrow to celebrate early with my mom's family. I'm still not really into the holiday spirit yet. I guess it's because things have been happening one thing after another and now that my meds are straight, I have to get sick with the stomach flu. I don't remember ever having such bad nausea! I'm just glad it's getting better and I'm hoping to be back to my normal strength before Christmas.

Chapter Seventeen

Winter 2004-2005

December 24, 2004

Holy hell, four years have gone by and I still have plenty of pages left to vent! We all went to Mass tonight as a family, including Philip for once, and Mike played his guitar in the choir. Then we went for a drive to look at Christmas lights.

Thankfully, I am finally over being sick, just in time for Christmas like I had prayed for. My appetite is somewhat back, so I am ready to feast tomorrow. This year we are having a smoked barbequed turkey that my daddy ordered from a restaurant, for a change, so they didn't have to slave away in the kitchen. Now all they have to do is nuke it and of course do the fixings on the side. I think Mom is fixing green bean casserole, mashed taters, biscuits, a Dutch apple pie, and Gamma is bringing a pumpkin pie, her homemade persimmon pudding, and her made-from-scratch sour dough rolls that are to die for.

This year is also another white Christmas. We had another snow storm that dropped seven inches of the white stuff a couple days ago. Good thing is it's packable. I can make snowmen, and we can have a snowball fight! It's also been very cold at night. Right now, it's one below, and with the wind chill, it's twelve below! I guess you can say it's colder than reindeer nuts!

In conclusion, this year couldn't be any better. Mike and I are finally able to be together on the holidays, and there are definitely more presents under the tree. I have a feeling there will be more when we wake up in the morning. That's usually how it works.

I'm going to snuggle up with Mike now in front of the fire. Merry Christmas to all and to all a good night!

January 8, 2005

Will this winter weather ever end? Now we are in the middle of an ice storm that began three days ago, but it feels like it's been much longer.

Today is Saturday, and we haven't had any power since 1:15 p.m. on Wednesday! My parents are too cheap to invest in a generator so we can at least have one TV going and lights in just a couple of rooms. They also won't invest in a kerosene heater so we can stay warm when we're not in the living room! I feel like we're Amish. The only difference is, we do have indoor plumbing, and fortunately, we are one of the only houses on the street with hot water because the water heater is gas as well as the stove.

Speaking of the stove, the funniest thing happened to my parents. The day the storm hit, they had just put an apple pie in the oven ten minutes before the lights went out, so that night we had that along with grilled cheese and fried tater cakes.

We have basically been camping out in the living room in our sleeping bags, and throughout the day, my daddy and I have been going around the neighborhood to see if anybody needs help with cutting tree limbs because we need the firewood. This is also when his three chainsaws come in handy the most!

When we're not doing that, we have been playing board games like Monopoly and Battleship and a hell lot of Uno! I've also colored so much I couldn't even tell you how many pages I've went through.

The thing that sucks the most is the fact that we couldn't go get Mike this weekend because yesterday we had four inches of snowfall on top of the ice, and the roads are slick again. I was looking forward to snuggling with him, and he always keeps my mind off the craziness! Now I'm stuck with nothing to do but stare at the four walls, all damn day, with nothing but the radio!

I pray the power comes back on soon so the sanity can be resumed to normal status! I can't stand it! I don't know how they did it back in the day! How did teens not go insane and kill each other? Yes, I know a lot of them had jobs and some of them already had kids, but the thought still wonders in my head on how the hell they survived, especially in the long, cold, hard days of winter!

January 31, 2005

God, why am I so damn stubborn? I'm definitely a spitting image of my daddy, but that's not always a good thing. I need to stop bottling up shit because a couple of weeks ago I was so stressed I decided to cut.

The insanity of no electricity and Mike telling me what to do and when to do it had built up to the point where I couldn't handle it anymore, and I didn't know how else to express my pain. I had been going to kickboxing regularly and exercising on the days I didn't do that, but still couldn't get rid of the emotional feelings. I now realize I should have written, but at the time, I didn't think that was even an option because of the overwhelming thoughts in my head.

The first two people to see it were my mom and my counselor. That was actually the day I did it, so we all talked, and I felt a little better. Then I had to tell Mike, and he told me if I ever did it again, he would never forgive me. When Grandma Sue found out after Amber saw them and shouted it to the world, she said she would turn me over her knee if I even ever thought about it again. Then when it finally got around in school, my teacher of record pulled me aside and gave me a lecture. She thinks I did it for attention, but she can believe what she wants to.

Onto other things now; today was the first day of second semester. Unfortunately, the dumb asses at school have put me back on diploma track. Now the pressure is back on there too. I guess I'm going to have to do the best I can because there's nothing I can do to change it!

February 8, 2005

Mike is still bossing me around like I'm his daughter. He always tells me to do my chores, and he calls to check if they are done. When they aren't, he bitches.

What happened to the old Mike? He used to be nice, and I miss the days where we were happy all the time. Will he ever be himself again? I don't know, but I will keep you posted.

Onto better things now; today is Fat Tuesday also known as Mardi Gras. That means, tomorrow is Ash Wednesday, also known as the official start of Lent. This will be a reminder to myself that as of tomorrow for the exception of Sundays, no sweets until Easter!

February 15, 2005

My teacher of record's mother died, so now we're stuck with a sub. It sucks because I miss her so bad. She's kind of like Mrs.

Fraley was to me but is not as close. Her class isn't nearly as small, and there are some things she does that I don't agree with, but she's still pretty cool.

Aunt Teresa and I are going to the mall in Castleton again this weekend. Grandma Karla gave her $50 to go toward a Build-a-Bear. I already have one that I made in Fort Wayne, but they're just so much fun to make. Then you get to dress them and make a birth certificate, so I'm starting a collection!

February 16, 2005

I know I just wrote yesterday, but I'm so bored it isn't funny. I didn't do a whole lot today besides go to school and go to the dentist to get x-rays of my wisdom teeth. I've got to get them out soon. My dentist is sending me to the oral surgeon so we can schedule.

My stomach has also been bothering me again. It has really never gone away since I was sick in December. The nausea went away, but I keep on having off and on deep gut pain. My doctor says its irritable bowel syndrome, but my question is why nothing I do seems to work?

My mental health on the other hand is good for now. I haven't had an episode for a couple of weeks. Knock on wood. Let's keep the good streak going!

March 8, 2005

I've been busy, busy, busy lately. Between kickboxing, school, and love life, it's a lot to handle!

I am gaining a whole lot out of kickboxing, strength being one of them. I'm also learning discipline and how to protect myself on the streets if necessary. Richard has also been picking me up and dropping me off because Mom doesn't want to, so now he's more like a second dad to me, and I call him Pappi. He's a great listener, and he gives great advice!

School is going OK, I guess. I have to retake the stupid I-Step test again because I failed it miserably last fall. They have also made the stupidest rule ever. We can't even have water bottles in class now. It's ridiculous! They need to enforce that rule to the teachers too! It's just water. We get thirsty too, and the water from the fountains is nasty. I also think they should put us on block schedule; that way lunch is longer and also make it so that we are allowed to go outside so we can burn off some of the excess energy that is built up during the school day. Unfortunately, with the assholes we have running the place right now, that will never happen!

My love life is pretty much the same. Mike is getting a little better as far as the bossing goes. He's still coming over every other weekend, but we are making the most with what we have.

March 16, 2005

I'm sitting here again after retaking the I-Step test. God, I hope I pass this time so I'm not stuck doing this again next fall! I'm sick of the same freaking routine every year! I pray as I do every time that I make it through this test in one piece!

Spring Break starts Friday. That's also the day I am having my wisdom teeth out, and depending on how I feel, I want to go up to Gampa and Gamma's house for a few days.

Mike is coming tomorrow, which is Thursday. It's also St. Patty's Day and our two year anniversary! I think we are going to just stay home and have a romantic evening!

Chapter Eighteen
Spring 2005

April 2, 2005

I have just received word that Pope John Paul II has died. From what I understand, he has been sick off and on lately. My family and I have been watching the news all afternoon, and we watched as many Catholics stood around St. Peter's Square in Rome. It's pretty sad because he's the only pope I have known.

Onto good things now; my parents, Mike, and I are going to a dance at church tonight; the dance is called the Spring Fling. They have a nice dinner and everything planned. I've got to get going because Mike is fixing to paint my toenails.

April 19, 2005

A new pope has been chosen. His name is Pope Benedict XVI

Mike finally lives in Muncie again! We are seeing each other almost every day now, and there are a lot of nights I stay at his house until Daddy gets off work and picks me up. It's so nice that we are happy again, and he's not bossing me around anymore.

The bad news about the situation is that he is only allowed thirty hours a week outside his house. However I am allowed to come over there pretty much any time. I'm glad his house manager is cool like that because not all of them in the company are.

Mom is going on one of her annoying streaks again. It seems like all she does nowadays is sit on her ass all day long, watch TV, and try to find something to bitch about. She almost never goes to kickboxing with me anymore, so either I have to get a ride with Mike and his staff or I have to call Pappi and pray that he has time to come pick me up. She claims she's too tired, but yet she hasn't done shit all day! God, I wish I could change her!

May 11, 2005

As you can see, I've still been busy. Since Mike has been back in town, I have been going non-stop! In fact, we went to prom a couple of weeks ago. Unfortunately, this year wasn't anything like last. The power went out and stayed out for two hours, so we had no music half the time. After prom was fun though. We got our caricatures drawn, and I got a much needed back massage!

In not so good news, Aunt Teresa and the asshole I used to call my uncle are no more! The good news, she was able to get away from him. Her and my cousin moved into a bigger nicer house in a great neighborhood, and the house even has a pool. That means, when I go there in the summer I will have a free place to swim now!

School is still going good. I'm just trying to hang in there because now we don't get out until June 13 because our school system doesn't know how to put built-in snow days into the school year calendar. It really sucks when all the other schools around are getting out for summer and we are stuck in here, wishing we were outside swimming or whatever! This is torture. I tell you, torture!

May 23, 2005

As of the fifteenth of this month, I am no longer a virgin. We have been using protection, but now that we're doing it, I'm freaking out that I'm going to get knocked up. I talked to my mom, and she reassured me that I should be fine because I'm on the pill and using the rubber.

In other news, I've been babysitting again, this time for my friends from church. Last Thursday, I watched their girls a few hours so they could go have dinner. Their six-month-old was teething and pretty much screamed the whole time. I tried to hold her change her burp her even feed her but she just continued. Then I put her in her swing, and she finally fell asleep for a little while. During that time, the three-year-old and I finger painted and colored. In the middle of coloring, the baby woke up again and, finally, wasn't screaming but crying, so I took care of her and put her to bed. Then I gave her big sister a bath because she had finger paint everywhere including her hair. After that, we read a bedtime story, and I tucked her into bed.

I just wish I could do that more often because of how good I am with kids. It also keeps my mind busy and gives me a chance to use my imagination. I do also know how to be a responsible adult. I know when somebody needs a time-out, how to cook, first aid, and all that good stuff. This is actually something I would like to do as a career someday after I finish school.

Speaking of school, I am so ready to get out now!

May 31, 2005

My life is officially over! Mike broke up with me yesterday morning and, of all things, had the balls to show up tonight at kickboxing just to see how I would react. He tried preaching to me after class, and I started crying hysterically. That's when Pappi stepped in and gave Mike a piece of his mind. Pappi had a very long talk with him and said that if he's going to start drama he is not welcome back! What would I do without Pappi? God love him!

June 17, 2005

Mike and I are finally back together after two weeks of not talking. I guess we just needed a break. He just came crawling back like a lost puppy, and I took him back in.

Now that things are good in that area of my life, my mom has decided to start being annoying again. She was OK for a few weeks, but now that it is finally summer and we're around each other more, she tries to find something to bitch about. She's always getting her panties in a bunch over the tiniest things that shouldn't matter. That's why she's miserable all the time. That's also what starts my parents' fights most of the time. She thinks Daddy hasn't done something right.

Please forgive my complaining. I know you want to hear about the good things, so here's it goes. The Shipman's annual activity is tomorrow. This year we're going to Indy to an Indians baseball game. I really wish we were going to Holiday World again or at least a state park. Baseball is like watching paint dry. I do, however, look forward to seeing my family.

Chapter Nineteen

Summer 2005

July 4, 2005

Happy Fourth of July! I was in Lafayette until today. Gampa and Gamma brought me back just in time for the fireworks. I went home with them from the other family reunion last Saturday at Princes Lakes.

Tomorrow, I have a doctor's appointment to check up on my meds, and Thursday, I am having surgery to stretch my bladder so I don't have to pee so much. I've been having problems ever since I had the really bad kidney infection in 2001. Thank God, I will only be restricted on my activity for one day. If it were any longer I think I would go nuts!

Mike and I are doing great. We hardly ever fight anymore, and when we do, we quickly make up. We never go to bed angry.

My pool is getting good use this summer as well. We swim pretty much every day unless it's storming. We invested in a new pump a few weeks ago because the one that came with the thing didn't pick up shit, and the water was green. Within a couple of hours of the new one being installed, we could see blue again, but it was still cloudy. It took a few days, but when all was said and done, it was as clear as the deep blue sea!

July 16, 2010

Today, my parents and I are packing our bags, getting ready for a fun-filled five-day camping trip to Shakamak State Park. We leave tomorrow after my cousin's birthday party in Fishers. This will be the first camping trip we have been on since I was five years old. I am so excited because, as you know, I like nature and camping, especially if nature is at its best!

The thing that sucks is Mike can't go with us this time because he's practicing for the Gus Macker. That's the big outdoor basketball tournament he is taking part in on next Saturday. We are coming back Friday so he can stay the night at our house, and we are taking him there Saturday morning.

July 19, 2005

I'm lying here in the tent after a long adventurous day. The park is huge. There are three lakes here, but the thing that sucks the most is we have to go fishing either very early in the morning or in the evening because it's so hot this week. It would be nice to have a camper with a little air but then again, that would just ruin the whole camping experience. My daddy is an Eagle Scout, and he can quickly adapt to any climate, while it takes me a little bit longer but not much. My mom, on the other hand, not surprisingly, complains she's too hot all the time.

OK, enough on the endless boring chatter and onto what we have been doing since we got here. We arrived on Sunday night at around nine thirty and picked out our campsite, which took a half hour. Then we set up the tent. That only took fifteen minutes, and after all that, we started settling down and Daddy started a campfire where we had some kettle corn. Let me tell you something; you haven't had anything until you have kettle corn over an open fire. Microwaves are so overrated.

Yesterday morning, we got up and drove to the camp store, checked out the main lake, hiked on a trail, then ended up getting so damn hot, so we dived into the pool. Our swim got cut way short because it started storming and wouldn't quit. That's when we went back to camp, and it had stopped raining for a while, so Daddy got another fire going for our dinner, which was "Hobo Pies." Right after he put the burgers on, it started pouring again, so we had to grab the portable camping stove!

This morning, we got up, and it was sunny and hot! We hit the pool and stayed there pretty much all afternoon, and my dumb ass put the tanning oil on and, instead of swimming like I usually do, I laid out part of the time, so now I have sunburn. After swimming, we were starving and I was tired, so we came back here. While Mom and Daddy ate dinner I came in here and crashed for forty-five minutes.

By the way, here's the recipe for "Hobo Pies":

✓ Carrots
✓ Potatoes
✓ Onions
✓ Hamburgers
✓ Buns! Don't forget them!
✓ Whatever other condiments you want!
✓ Aluminum Foil

You start out by getting your hamburger potatoes, carrots, and onions ready. Then wrap it in aluminum foil and cook it for a while. When that's done, add your bun and condiments and enjoy!

August 11, 2005

The rest of the camping trip was fun except for the last two nights. It stormed so bad that I ran and hid under the sink at the bathhouse across the road from our campsite. On the last night, it was so bad that I stayed in there two hours and the lights kept flickering. The storms kept on coming wave after wave. It would quit for ten or fifteen minutes at the most. Then the wind would start picking up; hail would start hitting the building really hard the lightning was fierce; and the rain came down in buckets! It was like the wrath of God! My mom finally came in to use the bathroom, and I scared the shit out of her. She convinced me to run back to camp with her and I did. I don't remember much after that until the next morning when we started packing up the camp. I'm just thanking God that we were on air mattresses because our tent had sprung a leak.

After the camping trip, I stayed home a week and then went down to Nut Nut's house in Jasper for another week. I was so dang busy there; I had no time to write. I helped her with her rural paper route, and we went swimming at her friend's house almost every day. We were also busy with vacation bible school at her church, so by the time we would get back to her house, it would be time to get ready for bed!

I'm just trying to enjoy my last week of freedom from the hellhole I call Muncie Central; just think though I'm a senior now! Just one more school year to go until I'm out of there!

August 28, 2005

Today is Katrina's seventeenth birthday, and what a coincidence! There's a category three hurricane getting ready to strike the Gulf coast in her honor! We made a little joke that she will forever be known from this day on as "Hurricane" Katrina! The name is perfect for her. She can be destructive at times and always tells it like it is.

My senior year, by the way, has started out on a good note. I have been working my ass off too. I'm even working on my first big project for sociology. For part of it, I have to get a certain amount of hours of community service, so, on September 17, I am helping Grandma Karla move into her new house.

September 10, 2005

I'm here at J-Fest again for my last year. It's been another long day of praise and Mike has been a complete asshole all day. This morning we had three workshops to choose from. I chose the one in the gym first, but Mike insisted on going to the one upstairs. That was fine, but when it came time for the break, I saw him hanging around some girl. Then the next session came around, and of course, he had to pick the one she went to instead of thinking of what I wanted. To be honest, she looks like one of the skanky whores that was in the psych hospital with me last time I was in there.

At this point, I'm not sure what to do. Do I stay with him? Do I ditch his ass? Or do we talk again? I just don't know. I guess all that's left to do is pray about it. I know God will show me the way!

Chapter Twenty
Fall 2005

October 4, 2005

A lot of shit has gone down since I last wrote. Mike and I had a long talk on that Sunday night after J-Fest. Things between us are much better now. I have also made it through the stupid I-Step test once again, and as I say every time, I hope to God I pass this time. If I didn't this time, I will have to be in a basic skills math class second semester, which will suck major ass.

In bad news, homecoming week this year started out shitty. On Monday morning, during first period, a kid whom of which I have known since the eighth grade asked his teacher for a pass to the nurse. Instead of going to the nurse, he somehow ended up going upstairs. He randomly went into an empty classroom where a girl was making copies for her aunt, who is a math teacher and grabbed her from behind with a knife to her throat.

The girl was able to grab the knife with her hand, but not before he had attempted to slit her throat. Thankfully, she survived with minor gashes to her hand and throat. She was treated with several stitches and released from the hospital the same day.

As for the punk, however he is now in juvie, awaiting trial. He is being charged with attempted murder and will possibly be tried as an adult.

October 24, 2005

I can't take this stress anymore! I thought my senior year was supposed to be fun. I think I'm failing in math. I am so burned out on homework and too pressured to pass all my classes to even think about having fun! Why did I have to fart around my freshman and sophomore years? I'm not ready to be eighteen yet! I don't want to grow up! My parents were cousins, and you know what they did!

November 11, 2005

My birthday was great. Mike and I had some dirty, kinky birthday sex. Then he took me to dinner at Outback Steakhouse, and after that, we went to the gas station so I could assert my independence and legally buy a pack of cigarillos.

Today, Mike came over after school, and we've been cleaning for the big party tomorrow, with my friends. I'm taking a short break right now because the sweeper keeps pissing me off.

December 17, 2005

It seems like I never have time to write anymore. I've been very devoted to my kickboxing. My mom has made me miss a class or two because she backed out at the last minute and it was too late to call Pappi, but either than that, I go to all the time.

I have also still been extremely busy with my schoolwork. It's paying off because I am finally getting all good grades!

Chapter Twenty-One
Winter 2005-2006

December 24, 2005

Well, another year has passed, and I haven't run out of pages yet. All I can say is that a whole lot has changed in five years. I have lost weight, grown taller and the rest of my body has taken its full womanly shape. My grades and attitude have also gotten much better and I am now in the best shape of my life.

The traditions are as usual this year. We all went to Mass this evening as a family, even Philip. Gampa and Gamma are of course coming tomorrow for lunch, which this year is ham because we couldn't afford the smoked turkey again this year. The only thing we are doing different is that Pappi will be picking up Mike and me for services at his church at 11:00 a.m.

Mike is going to love what I got him for Christmas. He's obviously been a good boy this year because this is what I got him: a Dale Sr. throw blanket, Dale Sr. framed picture, a Dale Sr. calendar and a Dale Sr. pocketknife!

Well, as I sign off, I'm going to say what I do every year! Merry Christmas to all, and to all a good night!

January 1, 2006

Happy New Year! I am so bored! Mike and I are just sitting here, trying to figure out what there is to do without money in this town. I can tell you, there's not much! I'm trying to save what I have left from Christmas, just in case I will need it later on, and you know how my parents are. They're way too stingy. It would be nice to get enough off them to at least go skating, but as we all know, that's a rare occasion.

Mike and I did have fun yesterday though. We went to one of the tattoo studios here in town and got our cartilage pierced, and while we were in there, waiting, we were looking at tattoo designs. I've decided that I'm going to get one when I get the money.

I got a ton of cool shit for Christmas by the way, even from my parents! The stocking stuffers are always the most fun. We never know what we're going to get, but we do know it's going to kick ass.

I think we finally decided we're fixing to take the dogs for a walk, so I've got to get going!

February 6, 2006

I'm getting busier and busier as the days go by. My parents are starting to drive me nuts with all the shit I have to get done before I graduate. I have to work my ass off in basic skills math because, you guessed it, I failed the math portion of the I-Step for the last time! I did pass English, however, which was a freaking miracle from the Lord himself.

Then they're telling me, immediately after graduation, I have to bust my ass to look for a job. I need some prayers on that because I've already filled out dozens of applications and I keep calling the places, but nothing is happening!

Speaking of prayers, I might be converting to Southern Baptist by the time I get married. We still don't have a wedding date set yet of course. We are just waiting for me to get school over with first. Then we will worry about all that good stuff!

February 20, 2006

Tonight is the first night of the youth retreat called Destination Jesus, and it's already been interesting. We started out with Mass followed by dinner. After dinner we jammed out to some awesome live praise music for an hour or so. Then we got into meditation and confession mode. By the time that was all said and done, it was time to break up into our groups, have night snack, and be bussed to our sleeping areas. Girls and guys separate of course. They made a rule at the retreat I went to in Kokomo a couple years back; girls are red, and guys are blue. What color do you get when you mix them together? Duh, purple, and there's no purple allowed the whole weekend!

Well, I better get going to bed. We have to get up at 5:30 a.m., and it's now one so nighty-night sleep tight; don't let the bedbugs bite!

March 7, 2006

The end of my senior year keeps on drawing closer and closer. Life is still busy, busy, busy as usual. I'm still in kickboxing and getting stronger as the weeks and months pass.

The rest of Destination Jesus, by the way, went really well. The attendance this year was the best in DJ's seven-year history. Seven hundred youth from not only the Diocese but also from across the country came. There was even a group all the way from Tennessee. I made some new friends as I always do, and I caught up with old ones too. I also came home with my hair braided again like I do with every retreat. I guess it's because when you get a bunch of us Catholic girls together, especially in our sleeping area, it's hard to fall asleep. We talk, do each other's hair and I've even seen some girls doing makeovers on each other. Basically, it's like a big sleepover!

In school news, Katrina dropped out a couple weeks ago. Supposedly, our child development teacher was accusing her of skipping class and spray painting the girls' bathroom. People that actually know Katrina know she wouldn't do such a thing. Unfortunately, the teacher believed the girls who tattled. In reality, it was those girls.

Chapter Twenty-Two

Spring 2006

April 10, 2006

I am so frustrated and burned out from school that, right now, it isn't funny. My stupid basic skills math class is harder than hell. My question is why in the hell do they expect us to know probability before we graduate? I'm just glad Mom and Daddy finally found me a tutor to help me through this shit! He practically has to do the problems for me.

In better news, Mike got a job at Pizza Hut. Tomorrow is his first day. I pray to God this job works for him because we are going to the prom again this year. Not only that, but he needs the money for other things as well.

April 17, 2006

    Philip is finally moving out today; oh yah, oh yah! He finally has his own apartment, so sayonara sucker! I finally have the house to myself with the exception of my parents, of course. No more phone calls asking for him 24/7; no more loogies in the sink; no more wash rags piled up on the towel rack, so that when I get in the shower there's no room for mine; and no more hogging up the computer!

    Onto other things, I forgot to tell you last time is that I am now on the Special Olympics swim team. I have already made some new friends, and some of my old ones are on the team already. In fact, my buddy Mitch, the one I had a crush on at one time, was the one who got me involved. I can't wait to compete in state games! It's June 2-4 in Terre Haute. I have finally found something I am good at. If only I had been able to join sooner!

May 15, 2006

    Graduation is in eleven days! The pressure is on to study so I can pass my finals! I so can't wait until the thirty-first!

    Today, I went to my counselor so she could go over the results of my psychological testing that Vocational Rehabilitation did a couple of weeks ago to see if I could get assistance with getting a job. She thinks I lied to make it seem like I am worse than what

I really am. I'm here to tell you that I didn't. The people asked me questions, and I told them how I felt. The results came back as me having bipolar and borderline personality disorder, which to me makes a lot of sense. That explains why I am always moody one minute, then can be on cloud 9 the next. Then other times, I have streaks where I'm really hyper and feel invincible, then hit rock bottom and can't even get up in the morning. That also explains the cutting and the extreme anger I have out of nowhere, but obviously, this counselor is a complete dumb ass and judges me by what she sees for just an hour. Now if she could only see me at home, that might change her mind!

I'm just glad I'm going swimming tomorrow so I can take my frustrations out on the water, and I really can't wait until state games! My goal is to win all medals, but if I don't it's all good. I will be having a great time with my friends.

May 31, 2006

I'm free! Free, I tell you! No more school! I made it! I wasn't sure if I would ever do it, but it's all done and over with now! Now to go out into the world and see what it has to offer! I'm going out first thing tomorrow to look for jobs. I'm going to be independent, damn it!

My open house isn't until June 11, but I am looking forward to it because I have invited a lot of my old friends and teachers, including Mrs. Fraley!

Before that though, I have state games to look forward to this weekend. I am so ready! I have been to every practice, and I've still been involved with kickboxing at the same time; so, if I wasn't in great shape before, I'm really in great shape now! I'm hoping to keep it that way too!

June 5, 2006

State games were great up until yesterday when I woke up sick with stuff coming out both ends. All together the whole experience was awesome. I finally found a group that I can belong to and be myself.

What I found really cool was that, between competitions, we could we could go to tent town which was out in a big parking lot. We could play games, have refreshments, and shop for souvenirs. We also had opening ceremonies on Friday night just like at the regular Olympics, and on our walk back, Mitch jumped into a bush full of poison ivy! Then on Saturday night, after dinner and out group pizza party, there was a dance.

How did I do, you ask? I got a gold in the twenty-five freestyle, a bronze in the fifty back, a silver in the twenty-five back, and a fourth place ribbon in the fifty breast. I would have gotten a silver medal in the breast, but when I did my wall turn, I swallowed water and slowed way down.

June 11, 2006

My open house was a success! Mrs. Fraley almost didn't make it in time, but she stayed after all the other guests left, so it was all good. We had a great turn out in attendance. A bunch of my old friends that I had invited that I hadn't seen in a while did show and that just made me happier than a pig in shit! The bad thing though was that nobody could go out and visit on the patio because today was shockingly cool and wet. That put a damper on my other idea. I was going to have a pool party with my friends, after the party. Damn Indiana weather! You know what they say about it though; if you don't like it, stick around five minutes, and it will change!

We didn't let the rain get in the way too much. Mike and I decided to go to the movies with Sierra and our friend Chris. He works at the theater so we got us a discount which was really nice. After that, Mike went home and I stayed the night with them at Chris's house.

Chapter Twenty-Three
Summer 2006

June 26, 2006

I've come to find out the real world is a bitch! I have been busting my ass, looking for a job, putting in applications everywhere, and still nothing! I think it's because I have no experience, and once the supervisors see that written down, they either push it aside or shred it into a million pieces.

On Thursday, I have an appointment with the job coach that Vocational Rehabilitation put me with. I'm hoping he will be able to help me. I really want to get out of my parents' house. They still ground me for God sakes. For example: At the present time, I'm not allowed to talk to Mike on the phone for the rest of the night and I can't have lunch with him tomorrow, simply because I forgot to take out the trash! I am eighteen, not eight! I wish this shit would stop! I know damn well if this were in Philip's case three years ago, they wouldn't ground him. They would just remind him not to forget again. And they wonder why I'm the rebel child? I want to be treated like an adult, damn it, but at this point, I'm not sure if that will ever happen at the rate we're going.

Speaking of bitching, here we go again. I've got to get going. Mom is bitching at me again. I wonder what I did wrong this time!

August 18, 2006

I know what you're thinking. Long time, no words, and I'm sure you're wondering what has been happening in my life, so here it goes. Mike and I got married on August 7 at the courthouse. We decided to just get it over with so he could have more freedom and so we could be together all the time like we want to. We are living with my parents now until he can find a better job outside the workshop. I am still working my ass off looking for work as well.

We are, however leaving for our honeymoon in Ft. Lauderdale, Florida, this coming up Tuesday and are staying seven days. We are really looking forward to it. This will be Mike's first time flying and his first time to Florida, and this will be the first time I have done something like this, partially on my own.

More good news, I finally got my driver's license, and I bought my first car an '85 Oldsmobile Cutlass. I named her the Tasmanian Devil because she's fierce and you can hear her coming down the road!

August 25, 2006

I'm just sitting here in our hotel room after another really great day at the beach. Yesterday, we met a couple from up-state New York (Bob and Mandy). They came here to find work, and they don't have any money with them, so we did what Jesus would do and bought them dinner last night. Then this morning at about 9:00 a.m., we had a knock at the door and wouldn't you know it!—they came back. That's when we went to the beach and cooled off the rest of the afternoon. After that, we ate at the restaurant deck here and then Mike and I decided to open up our room to Bob and Mandy since the last couple of nights they've had to sleep on the beach. Now they are asleep on the floor and Bob is snoring like a chainsaw!

Yesterday was also the day Mike and I rented bikes. We hadn't even had the damn things fifteen minutes and I slammed on my brakes too hard to avoid a car and flipped completely over the handlebars! I ended up on the ground with one of them in my thigh, so now I have a hideous bruise to show. After that ordeal, we walked the bikes back to the hotel and caught the bus to the mall, where we shopped for a while, and I went and got my hair highlighted. Then on our way back to the hotel, we stopped at a tattoo shop, and you guessed it! We got matching tattoos. I got it on my calf, and he got it on his upper arm.

Chapter Twenty-Four
Fall 2006

November 4, 2006

Married life is keeping me on my toes. It's obvious because as you can see I haven't written in two and a half months.

Here's what's going on in my life, today was our bowling tournament for Special Olympics. I got fourth place. Mike was involved, but he dropped out for some reason. We also picked up our newest family member today. Her name is Lucy, she's thirty-two pounds; she's a Kelpie mix, and she howls. If you haven't guessed, she's a dog!

Next Saturday is Mike and my wedding reception, and that night, he will be fighting in the annual King of The Ring fights that Pappi puts on.

That brings me to my next subject. I don't know what has gotten into him since we got married. He got us kicked out of my parents' house once for cussing my mom out, and he's being an ass toward everybody lately.

In even worse news, I had a job from September to October that lasted three weeks, working with kids at a daycare center with two year olds. I was with ten of them at once, and I ended up having a meltdown, so I got fired. Now I'm back to square one, busting my ass putting in applications everywhere, hoping to God somebody hires me, since I've lost touch with my job coach. Mike, on the other hand, has a job selling vacuums. Unfortunately, that's not working too well either. Nobody wants to buy them because the damn things are too expensive!

In some much better news, my parents, Mike, and I went to see Gretchen Wilson in late September. Her show kicked ass, and she saved her best song for last. "Redneck Woman" was her encore finale. She had her fans make some noise. Then she came back out rocking, and it was great!

November 11, 2006

The wedding reception today went great as planned. We were even able to get some awesome pictures outside, even though it was damp and cold the whole time. We had a good turn out on our guest list, meaning three-fourth of the people showed.

The bad news is Mike is still being an ass. He keeps taking off with the car and he has no driver's license. The worse thing about it is he never lets me go with him like he has something to hide. Now I'm really starting to regret marrying the son of a bitch! I didn't realize how self-centered he was until the honeymoon was over. I wish somebody would have warned me of some of his games before because I definitely would have given it a second thought!

As for the fight tonight, he lost. He wasn't in the ring even ten seconds and his knee gave out. I don't know why he even decided to fight this time around anyway, knowing this would probably happen anyway. Oh, I know, he wants to be a dumb ass as usual and show off. That's how he injured the damn thing in the first place by playing basketball with a bunch of kids that were way younger than him. God, he is so stupid!

November 28, 2006

The bullshit keeps getting worse and worse. He took away my cell phone just because I wasn't answering. He didn't believe me when I said I don't hear it all the time. Come to find out he gave it to his dickweed ass friend. My question is, "What the hell makes him more special than me," and to top that all off, Mike is still driving my car with no license. It's worse now than ever. He's taking it and just comes and goes as he pleases. I never know when he's coming home, and when he does, he reeks of pot and demands a piece of ass, and I have to give it to him because he locks the bedroom door and won't let me out until

I do. Sometimes, he stays the night. If he does, he gets up in the morning, eats, and takes off again!

At this point, I am too scared to say anything to my parents because I fear what he will do to me. I really pray I can somehow get away from this situation soon. It hurts mentally and physically. When I tell him to stop, he just tells me to shut up and calls me a pussy, and for the fear of my life, I do as I'm told but at the same time pray silently that it's over with soon.

December 10, 2006

Mike is finally starting to take me with him, but all they really do is sit around and smoke pot all day, but I guess I do have some fun talking to the girls over at the house he is staying at, and we did go on a cigarette run the other night and we ran into Eric Estrada.

You're probably wondering how in the hell that's possible in Muncie, so I'm here to explain. For the last couple of weeks, CBS has been shooting a reality show with the Muncie Police Department. They have trained five celebrities—Eric Estrada, Wee Man, Jack Osborne, Trish Stratus, and Latoya Jackson—to be cops, and now they are protecting the city of Muncie, with camera crews following closely behind in a black van. That's how you know when one of them is in the car is if the van is right behind it.

The first episode airs on January 10 at 8:00 p.m.! I can't wait because it's not every day you see Muncie, Indiana, on TV!

Also in the spotlight, the Indianapolis Colts are doing great this year. They haven't lost but one game. This is actually my first year of really paying attention to NFL football, and it's actually kind of interesting. I think the Colts might just make it all the way to the Super Bowl. They are doing the best job I ever recall!

Chapter Twenty-Five
Winter 2006-2007

December 24, 2006

Wow, six years now, and as you know, I have changed a lot. We're going to midnight Mass this year and as usual, there are a ton of presents under the tree. There is, however, a change in tradition in the case of Gamma and Gampa. Instead of them coming to our house on Christmas Day, all the Shipmans are getting together New Year's Day at Golden Corral in Bloomington. There's also no snow again this year. They are predicting another mild winter. It sucks ass!

Mike is finally hanging around again. I'm just wondering how long it will last. I think he might just be using us for the free food and presents, but let's not jump to conclusions. I will keep you posted.

Well, there's not much else I have on my mind, so I will sign off as I do every year. Merry Christmas to all and to all a good night!

January 3, 2007

My suspicions were correct. He was just using us. He's back to his old tricks again! He won't tell me where he's going; I'm not allowed to go with him; and he's coming and going as hediddly damn well pleases with my car again! When Mike is here, he makes Lucy nervous, and when she piddles, he puts her in the cage for hours at a time, and if I try to let her out, he throws a bitch fit because she's supposed to be in "big trouble"!

Like I've said before, I wish there was a way to get away from his crazy ass before things get even worse, and he beats the shit out of me. He already does it to Lucy and wonders why she bites him! I'm so scared for my life, and I don't know what to do. It pisses me off. I still don't feel like I can tell anybody because of the way he will react. It's hard telling what he is capable of. The man is a monster. I hate him. Why did I even get with this bastard?

January 17, 2007

I have finally found a safe haven for us to go! Grandma Karla has opened up her home in Martinsville. That's one hundred miles away from Muncie and the bullshit drama that's in it! It couldn't have come at a better time either.

You see, my parents left for Hawaii a couple of days ago, and I decided to go to my friend Beth's house to stay the night. Well, I realized I had forgotten something at my house, so we went back to get it. The moment I walked in the door, Mike started in on me saying that I wasn't supposed to be there and shit. He was even stupid enough to call my parents that night when he knew they were already asleep because they had an early flight in the morning.

Now Beth and I are at Grandma's until next Wednesday. That's the day my parents get back. Then I'm going back to Muncie, packing my shit, and leaving. I know it's going to be hell, but I got to do what I got to do. He's had way too many damn chances, and he has blown them.

The good news, I will be joining the Special Olympics basketball team here. The first practice is Sunday; it's great timing! I'm really hoping to make new friends again because it can be hard for me sometimes. This will also be the first time I have lived outside of Muncie, so I'm not sure what to expect?

January 21, 2007

My first day of basketball was fun. The disadvantage is that there are only four girls in the whole group. They have separated us all onto four different teams too, so now we are playing with all guys, and they are quick!

In other news, there is finally snow! My friend Brooke and I built snowmen this afternoon before the big AFC South Championship game, which was Colts versus Patriots! The Colts won, which means they are going to the Super Bowl! However, there is a conflict—the Bears are also going to Super Bowl! Why is it my two favorite teams are playing each other in the Super Bowl? Oh well, I still say Colts all the way baby, February 4 in Miami!

January 27, 2007

I don't know why, but I'm giving dumb ass one more chance. I guess it's because when he heard that I was leaving he got down on his knees and begged me not to go. It's pathetic, I know, but I gave him the benefit of the doubt because I'm so damn nice. I did, however lay his ass on the line and told him straight up that if he screws up this time, I will be gone for good. No questions!

Lucy and I still made the move down here to Martinsville, but with Mike with us. He has promised to work on his GED and promised he would give his life to Christ.

I'm just curious to see how this will all work out. Will he really change this time? Or is he putting on another show? We will just have to play it by ear I guess.

February 4, 2007

The Colts have done it! They will now forever be known as Super Bowl XLI champions, February 4, 2007! In my daddy's face! He's pissed because the Bears are his no. 1 favorite team and they lost to the Colts for once!

We just got done cleaning up from the big party we had too. We had plenty of snacks including cupcakes with blue icing. Unfortunately, I haven't been able to eat too much for some odd reason. I have been nauseous a lot lately, and I have had the Hershey squirts the last three days. The worst thing about all this is I'm off all my meds because yesterday I went to the doctor and they did a urine pregnancy test, but the results were inconclusive, so they got blood from me. Hopefully the results come back soon because I need to know if I am I need to see my doctor so she can get me on meds that are safe to take. I'm kind of hoping I am, but on the other hand not. We are definitely not financially stable at this point.

February 6, 2007

My results came back, and I was pregnant. Unfortunately, ten minutes after I got the phone call letting me know, I went to the bathroom and passed a big clot. That's when Grandma decided it was a smart idea to take me to the hospital to see what was going on. When we got there, they did both tests and found out I had in fact miscarried.

I was only five and a half weeks, but it still makes me very sad. The baby was a part of me. I was actually starting to look forward to changing diapers and getting up for nighttime feedings. I guess we are just going to have to try again!

February 23, 2007

I'm slowly returning to my normal self, but there hasn't been a whole lot to do to keep us occupied lately because we had a blizzard a week ago and everybody is still trying to dig out. Mike and I can't convince Grandma to let us go sledding. She's afraid we're going to get hurt, and we have no insurance, so we've been playing out in the snow at the house.

Right now, we are on our way to Muncie, so I can talk to my doctor about putting me on meds that are safe for pregnancy.

In other news, I forgot to tell you that when my parents were in Hawaii, there house was robbed, and I have a feeling Mike has something to do with it. After all, he was the one who told me to get out of my own house. That might be when he was staging it?

The sad thing is they took shit that was very valuable to all of us. The first thing to come up missing was Mom and Daddy's safe deposit box. Then the other things including the Kirby sweeper that Mike sold us, two of my daddy's chainsaws, an antique rifle passed down from my great-grandfather from WWI, my mom's gold watch, some of my daddy's tools, three of my DVDs, and we keep on stumbling upon more things as we go. All I know is that whoever is responsible, when found, there will be hell to pay!

March 17, 2007

Mike is finally handing his heart over to the Lord. He and I are being baptized tomorrow at Grandma's church, meaning I will no longer be Catholic, but Protestant. I also now have a Christian godmother. Her name is Lou Ann, and I think God sent me to her as my guardian angel because she is there for me whenever I need her.

Also going on tomorrow is the family get-together for the March birthdays, so most of them will be here just in time for the service. Then we will be going back to the house for dinner and all the other good stuff that goes along with the party.

Chapter Twenty-Six

Spring 2007

March 23, 2007

Great news! I am pregnant again! I'm only four weeks, but this one feels completely different from the last. I'm definitely looking forward to my first ultrasound and hearing the baby's heartbeat. The freakiest thing about my due date is that it's November 15. That's exactly twenty years to the day my mom was due for me. That would be so cool if I had the baby on my birthday.

In other news, Mike and I are moving back to Muncie because he got a job at Target, with my mom. He starts work on April 1. No April fool. It's for real, and I'm looking forward to moving back. I'm really hoping he can keep this job so we can find our own place. I want to raise this baby as a couple and not live with my parents, if it's all possible by the time this baby comes.

May 7, 2007

My baby is alive! I had my first ultrasound today. The heartbeat was great, and the baby was even sucking its thumb. The doctor is concerned, however, about the thickness on the back of the neck. He recommended that I have an amniocentesis. That's where they take fluid from the baby, with a needle that goes into my belly, to test for genetic abnormalities. I'm kind of freaked out. A needle in my belly is not going to feel too good. I have gas built up and it hurts all the time as it is, but I guess I will tough it out for the baby.

Onto the bad things in life now; Mike got fired from Target after two weeks because he's a lazy ass. He also missed my appointment today because he was hanging out with his buddy; so at this point I'm not sure what to do with him. I know if he keeps on screwing around with his friends again and totally blowing me off, I will be gone!

May 23, 2007

The amniocentesis was today, and, not surprisingly, the jackass I call my husband didn't show again. Thankfully, my mom was there. It was scary, and I'm glad it's over with. Now to anxiously wait for the results, which I'm hoping to come back as showing the baby is just a carrier of the chromosome abnormality like me but only time will tell. This will also determine the sex. I'm hoping for a girl, but I will take whatever.

Back on the subject of Dib Shit, he is once again going back to his old ways. He's hardly ever around anymore, and I have come to the conclusion that he's running around on me. I also think there might be drugs involved.

When I get my chance to escape this time, I am not looking back. He has changed so much. He just wants me for money and sex. I should have seen it before, but I was blinded by his so called "love." I now know I should have listened to my friends, especially Katrina. My teachers also warned me of his games, but no, I had to be a dumb ass and fall for him. Now, I'm suffering. He has spent almost all of my inheritance I got from my great-grandparents and has drained me of all other funds.

I have got to get away from him soon, or he will surely kill me. He's a stupid coward and needs to be locked up in the mental institution for life!

May 27, 2007

I am worried sick. I'm bleeding, and when I say that, I mean two pads a day. Mike took me to the ER last night when it started. I was babysitting for a friend, and my stomach started hurting. I thought it was gas as usual, but when I got up to use the bathroom, I felt something warm gush out down there. I quickly ran in there and saw that I was bleeding. I immediately tried calling the ~~Dib~~ Shit on his buddy's phone, and no answer. I called five more times and nothing, so I had to wait until he finally got back an hour and a half later. When he finally got there and I told him, he started going off on people for no reason. Then he drove me to the hospital and dropped me off, then farted around with his buddy some more, just like I wasn't important. He finally came back about two hours later and stayed with me for a while, but took off again before the nurse came in with the fetal Doppler to hear the baby's heartbeat. Then when they finally discharged me I had to wait on him for another hour!

It's obvious he thinks his friends are more important than his pregnant wife. Now he's gone again. He's in Ohio, supposedly doing a construction job, but I haven't seen a penny from it. I think him and his buddy are dealing drugs to be honest, but whatever. I don't and won't be a part of it.

May 30, 2007

Today, I got the worst news an expectant mother wants to hear. My baby didn't make it. I went in for another ultrasound today because I'm still bleeding, and even before I went to the appointment, I had a feeling something wasn't right.

When the nurse took me back to the room, she had the on-call doctor to give me the results of the amniocentesis. That's when

I got the news that the baby did in fact have the chromosome abnormality. I then asked what the sex was. She was happy to tell me it was a boy. I was so excited to hear the news. That's also when I chose the name Joel David, but the joy was short lived.

As soon as the nurse put the probe on my belly, I kept looking at the screen and looking back at her. The look on her face was very concerning. The baby appeared to be head down, and he wasn't moving. Then after a while, she went and got the doctor and they checked for a heartbeat and there was no sign of life. That was when they told me the doctor was going to have to do a D and C to get him out. It's scheduled for June 8 at 1:00 p.m.

I started bawling because I knew I had the daunting task of telling Mike the bad news, and when I did finally work up the courage to call him, he said I was lying and hung up on me. Then he had the balls to call back cussing me out, saying that I killed his baby!

June 8, 2007

Joel is now gone for good. May his soul rest in peace, for I know I will see him again someday, and the saddest thing is that I'm lactating and there's no baby to feed.

I feel like shit, and I hardly ever feel like getting off the couch anymore. Dickweed is still in Ohio and obviously doesn't give two shits about me, so now the only thing I have are my family and friends to help me through this hell of a time.

June 17, 2007

That asshole has violated me for the last time! He came home today, demanding a piece of ass, as usual, and I told him no and that it hasn't been two weeks yet since the D and C, and I'm not healed yet.

Instead acting like a human, he acted like an animal, grabbed me by my hair and threw me onto the bed. He then made me jack him off until he cummed, then made me eat it. After that, he forced himself on top of me and I told him to stop, that it hurt, but he continued and called me a pansy.

By the time he finally unlocked the door and we got into the shower I couldn't even look at him. I let him go before me, so I didn't have to deal with him for that much longer. As I went to pee and when I got out of the shower I was gushing blood.

I am too scared to tell my family again. I am scared for not just my life, but my family's life as well. He's gone psycho I tell you!

Chapter Twenty-Seven

Summer 2007

I don't know how to escape from Mike. I'm afraid to leave because I'm not sure what he will do. I have a feeling he would track me down and try to get me back, and because he has that much control over me, I probably would fall for his tricks once again.

Last night is the perfect example of this man's power over me. He dragged me to his friend's house where there was no power and no food. We stayed the night there, and when we woke up this morning he took a shower which was totally pointless because it's ninety-five degrees in the shade. After he got out of the shower I was just sitting there burning up and hungry, but all the selfish jackass does is look at me and start scraping the resin out of a broken marijuana pipe.

As we finally got into the car I thought we were going back to my parents' house, but no! He is so damn desperate for pot money he had to pawn off one of his stupid guitars. We ended up running to two pawn shops and even one of his drug buddies, which is where he wouldn't let me out even though I was extremely thirsty, and because he wouldn't let me turn on the air I was so hot I thought I was going to die of heat exhaustion.

By the time he finally gave up, it was 3:30 p.m. I was dehydrated, hungry, and so pissed that I couldn't even see straight! It makes me furious that he cares more about his damn pot than his wife when he knows damn I am still lactating and bleeding. He also knew that my shirt was soaked with breast milk, and as usual, he didn't give two shits, as long as he was happy.

All I've got to say is there's no place like home and I can't be any more relieved to be back here in the cool air and with Lucy by my side. The pool has also never felt better. I jumped in this afternoon and stayed for two hours, and I'm going again tomorrow.

June 27, 2007

Lucy and I are once again free women! Mike walked in two nights ago after getting the car towed for the third time, and he immediately started in on another rampage. He said he had called the doctor and found out I punched myself in the stomach to kill the baby, and as we all know, that's bull shit. I would never do such a thing!

That had been the final straw. As soon as Mike took off again, Daddy came out of his bedroom and said that he had heard everything. Shortly after Mom, Daddy, and I all sat down in the living room and started to discuss my options. We quickly decided to call Grandma and give her the heads up that I was coming the next day because it was Sunday, and we had to get my car out of hawk, so I started packing my shit once again.

Yesterday, as Daddy and I were leaving to get the car thing taken care of, we saw Dickweed riding his bike toward my parents' house. I'm not sure what he was planning; either he was going to butter me up and apologize as usual or he was going to start hell. It ended up he raised hell and called the cops on my mom. He told them my parents kidnapped me, and they just laughed at him. I cracked up when I heard it too! They did, however, make him give Mom her house key back before he was escorted off the property!

Now Lucy and I are starting our new lives—asshole free! I still have to get my medicines straight, but with the help of Grandma and my friends here, it will go a whole lot easier. I also have the help of the Lord. I still pray and meditate all the time!

July 4, 2007

I am still overwhelmed with my emotions. My doctors say it's partially postpartum depression but also my bipolar. She finally took me off my Zyprexa and put me back on Lithium, but I am still crying over nothing. I guess I'm going to have to take it day by day again.

It's still been hard for me to get the motivation to get up and exercise. I have been trying to go to the YMCA when I can, now that I have a membership. I get it free because Grandma and I volunteer by babysitting on Thursday nights for them. That keeps me a little busy, but not for long enough. I'm trying to find something that does because I want to start feeling better mentally and physically.

As for the Fourth of July fireworks today, we went to the celebration in New Castle, and it got postponed at the last minute because it started pouring ten minutes before the show and didn't stop until midnight. Now we have to wait until Friday night. Mom said she probably wouldn't go. Good for her! That just means no bitching! She always bitches, and it starts shit between my parents when they're in the car together. It never fails.

July 11, 2007

I'm starting to feel better mentally, but, physically, still not so great. Every time I eat, my stomach starts hurting, and I'm constantly having the Hershey squirts. What really makes no sense is I'm gaining weight like hell, even though I'm barely eating. I'm pushing two hundred pounds. I've never been this damn big and I just keep gaining and gaining and gaining! It makes me want to starve myself for months on end! I even get so mad sometimes that I want to stab myself in the stomach so I don't have to suffer anymore.

I'm not going to be fat! I hate this feeling, and I'm getting stretch marks all over to make things worse. I want to feel like I did before I got married, when I got out of high school! I feel so ugly now! I'm hideous!

Today was my cousin's graduation from Ball State, and my parents and I went. Being in the big crowd was pretty overwhelming, but I made it. My mind, however, was racing the whole time.

Gampa and Gamma were also there, which brings me to my next worry. Gamma has been having bad stomach pain lately and has also been very weak. She has been to the doctor a couple of times, but they still don't know what is wrong, and this morning before the ceremony even started, she had another episode. I've never seen her so pale and in so much pain before. Thankfully, it went away and she did OK for the rest of the day, but I am still worried about her. She doesn't look good.

August 11, 2007

Gampa just called Daddy and told him Gamma just got out of surgery to repair a perforated bowel. God knows why in the hell it took so damn long to figure that out. It shouldn't take a genius, especially when her stomach was so bloated; she couldn't shit, and she was puking all the time. They should have recognized something wasn't right when Gamma's stomach looked like she was nine months pregnant, when she is usually skinny.

They finally did a CAT scan last Thursday and saw that her stomach was full, so they pumped it and, instead of admitting her and doing further testing, they sent her home. Gampa said she felt better until last night. She made it until noon or so today and had another episode. That's when they went back to the hospital and did another CAT scan and discovered that there was a mass on her pancreas that had perforated her bowels.

Now, she is currently in intensive care, and we are waiting for the results from the biopsy that the doctor took of the mass. We are going up to see her tomorrow.

August 17, 2007

Gamma is now on life support. She is in very grave condition. We have been up at the hospital all day every day since the twelfth. It's hard to see her like this, with the tube in her nose, the ventilator and all the other stuff hooked up to her.

We know she is sick! Gamma is tough; she's a fighter! You almost never hear her complain. That was until about a month ago when we saw her at my cousin's graduation. She's usually very active—cleaning the house regularly, doing laundry every day, and taking walks with Gampa. This is a shock. It is all happening so fast. Just a couple months ago, she was her normal self. It's funny how fast things can change.

August 21, 2007

It's been a long and hard day for the Shipman family. Gamma died at 11:41 a.m., surrounded by the whole family. We decided the other day that she wouldn't be happy living like a vegetable, so we set the meeting time of 9:15 a.m. this morning so we could be together as a family to say our good-byes and be at her bedside as we pulled the plug as she took her last breaths.

Tomorrow, I am going with Gampa, Daddy, and Aunt Clarice to do the daunting task of making arrangements for the funeral Mass. They said something about making it on Saturday so people don't have to miss work on Monday.

In other news, Mike is trying to get back with me. Trust me, it's not going to happen. He's too much of a Dib Shit!

Chapter Twenty-Eight
Fall 2007

November 1, 2007

Sorry, it's been forever since I last wrote. I've been sick and then I was busy and haven't had a chance so here's what has happened.

Gamma's funeral was on August 24. A week after that Aunt Teresa and I went to Six Flags in St Louis. Unfortunately, on the way back, I felt sicker than a dog. I thought I was going to puke for sure but thankfully never did.

For the next couple of weeks, the nausea still wouldn't subside and I was having the Hershey squirts right along with it. When I finally went to go see my doctor in Muncie, she ordered an ultrasound and a scan of my gallbladder with dye. When I got the call back that the results showed nothing, I was furious. I knew something was wrong, and the next time

I went back to my doctor, she told me that whoever read those results were wrong. She referred me to a surgeon down here in Martinsville. By the time I was scheduled for surgery, it was October so I had suffered for a month.

When I finally did have my surgery, however I started feeling better. At first, I was in a lot of pain. When I first woke up from anesthesia, I was in tears. I couldn't walk straight for a week, let alone laugh, sneeze, cough, or fart.

After a week of Lou Ann spoiling the crap out of me and being there a whole bunch, I asked her to pick me up for the last day of Special Olympics bowling on a Saturday. That morning, I woke up to see Grandma on the toilet, not being able to get up. She had been there all night, and I didn't know what to do, so I waited for Lou Ann to get here. We ended up having to call the ambulance, and she was admitted for a couple of days for her arthritis.

During that time, Lou Ann took me to bowling as planned. Then we went out to eat lunch, and after that, we went back to her house, and she invited me to stay the night. We had so much fun because later that evening we went to a bonfire at one of her friend's house.

Last but not least on my list, last Friday, I went to my friend Courtney's Halloween slumber party. Then on Saturday morning, I woke up at the ass crack of dawn to compete in the Fall Classic. The annual state fall meet for Special Olympics Indiana. I got a silver medal, a gold medal, and a fifth place ribbon. They were all relays.

November 11, 2007

I am now twenty! I can't believe how fast the time goes. Lou Ann took me out to dinner for my birthday and went to Wal-Mart afterward, where she got me a movie.

Today, we celebrated the family November birthdays down here, and that's when I got some really sad news. Jake attacked another dog. This time it was our close neighbors' that we consider more like family.

It happened yesterday afternoon when Daddy was coming out of the gate. Jake saw Molly and charged toward her. She survived but had serious wounds similar to the ones of his last victim. Now it's for sure that Monday morning Daddy has the daunting task of taking Jake to the place of no return.

I am going to miss him. He was playful and so full of life, but on the other hand, we can't have this happen again because it's like Jeff said, "What if that would have been Kylie?" That's the neighbors by the way. It's not worth risking humans over a stupid dog!

November 22, 2007

Happy Turkey Day! Wow, I had two Thanksgiving dinners this year lunch with Grandma's family in Indy and then up here to my parents' house, where I am now stuffed and watching the Colts versus Lions game; Colts are leading, of course!

I couldn't be happier at the moment, and for once, it feels like November outside. The high temperature only made it to thirty-two degrees today. Daddy just fired up the fireplace an hour ago, so I am definitely staying nice and toasty.

Later this weekend, I get to help Mom and Daddy put their Christmas stuff up. I'm already into the holiday spirit, but I can't wait until Grandma and I put up ours!

December 9, 2007

Doggone it! I hate my body! I have the stomach flu and now I can't go with my parents and Gampa to Kansas City for my great-aunt and uncle's golden wedding party. They left today, and I'm stuck here at home, doing nothing but having the Hershey squirts, puking, and watching boring TV reruns!

I've got to get better soon so I can hang out with Lou Ann and we can go back to the YMCA. There is one bonus. I was feeling good enough today to have my neighbor help me make my Colts blanket. It wasn't too hard, but I know with my deep perception that I would have never been able to do it without her.

December 20, 2007

I'm in the hospital again. The doctor has put me on Depakote, and it seems to be working great. I am actually sleeping at night. He also prescribed something for my stomach that works wonders, and I am now able to eat without shitting afterward.

I haven't felt this good since high school, except for the fact that I wish I could lose some of this god-awful weight. I'm up to 215 pounds now, and I hate getting on the scales anymore. I know it's going to be higher than last time, and it seems like no matter how much I exercise I can't get rid of it. Unfortunately, I think it's these meds. I wish they could put me on something that didn't have this horrible side effect!

The weight gain is what brought me in this time. I was feeling so bad about myself that I wanted to grab a butcher knife and stab myself in the stomach like I had written in the past, but this time, I was serious. I was sick of looking at my reflection in the mirror.

Now I'm just hoping and praying that the team of doctors, therapists, and group therapy can help me get rid of these horrible feelings and I can replace them with positive coping techniques. I'm also hoping to get out of here before Christmas, but if I don't, it's OK!

Lou Ann and Grandma have been coming to see me every day. They brought me my blanket, and Lou Ann even bought me a little frog with reindeer antlers to make me smile. She also brought me a twenty-four pack of crayons and a couple of coloring books to keep me busy during my free time. My favorite group by the way is arts and crafts.

Chapter Twenty-Nine

Christmas 2007

December 24, 2007

Wow, seven years have come and gone, and I'm finally on my last entry. I'm out of the hospital now and feel more like myself again.

I am currently at my parents' house, and we are planning to go to midnight Mass, which is here in about an hour. Tomorrow, we are having Christmas dinner, just Grandma, my parents, Philip, and me. This year is the same as last with Shipmans, except this year instead of meeting at Golden Corral we are going to a Pizza place.

Well, I guess, since this is the ending entry, I should make it memorable, so here it goes! I guess we can look back at all the times my mom and I got into it and were cool a couple days later or all the times Katrina and I were enemies, but we ended up staying friends all this time. We are one hundred miles away, but that doesn't stop us from using the phone.

Everybody will always remember September 11 and the heroes that died that day and that most want Bin Laden dead. If you will remember I gave you the 411 on the torture me and my daddy recommend.

Don't even get me started on the douche bag I call my soon to be ex-husband! I don't know how in the hell I got with him in the first place. I met him in my freshman year and I guess I was so desperate that I fell for his stupid tricks!

My days in the high school youth group were a blast! The youth retreats were always the highlight of the years, right along with the scavenger hunts and movie night! Oh, and I think I forgot to mention that one weekend when we went on that camping trip with them, and Katrina, me, and a bunch of the other girls got the Hershey squirts because of the greasy walking tacos we had that night! Boy, was that Imodium ever so handy!

On a serious note, let's not forget all who have died in the past seven years including the two kids from school who were involved in the New Year's Day 2004 crash, Chris's two brothers, Grandma Becca, Gamma Shipman, and, especially, my son Joel. I ask God may all their souls rest in peace!

I also recently found out that I do in fact have bipolar borderline personality disorder. It was charted by the doctor at the hospital. This explains everything! This explains me, and that's why I say, "Don't open your mouth until you have lived a day in my shoes!"

Things to Always Remember

- Don't worry, be happy!
- Never wear shoes in the summer!
- Only listen to your mom if she bitches all the time and you feel that it is super important!
- Pray at least once a day!
- Brush your teeth twice a day!
- Shower regularly!
- Bug your siblings as needed!
- If you are a daddy's girl like me, hang out with him when possible!
- Listen to your favorite music loudly and proudly!
- Always be yourself! You will be surprised how far you can really get!

Edwards Brothers, Inc.
Thorofare, NJ USA
August 24, 2011